C000080646

Scribe Publications
ON OFFENCE

Richard King was born in 1971 in England, and now lives in Fremantle, Western Australia. He is a freelance writer and has a master's degree in literary history. Richard writes and reviews books for *The Australian* and *The Sydney Morning Herald*, as well as for numerous journals and magazines, including *Australian Book Review, Meanjin, Overland, PN Review Poetry London, Quadrant, Southerly,* and *The London Magazine.*

ON OFFENCE

THE POLITICS OF INDIGNATION

RICHARD KING

SCRIBE

Melbourne • London

Scribe Publications Pty Ltd
18–20 Edward St, Brunswick, Victoria 3056, Australia
50A Kingsway Place, Sans Walk, London, EC1R 0LU, United Kingdom

First published by Scribe 2013

Copyright © Richard King 2013

All rights reserved. Without limiting the rights under copyright reserved above,
no part of this publication may be reproduced, stored in or introduced into
a retrieval system, or transmitted, in any form or by any means (electronic, mechanical,
photocopying, recording or otherwise) without the prior written permission of the
publishers of this book.

While every care has been taken to trace and acknowledge copyright, we tender apologies
for any accidental infringement where copyright has proved untraceable and we welcome
information that would redress the situation.

Typeset in 12/17 pt Adobe Caslon Pro by the publishers
Printed and bound in Australia by Griffin Press

The paper this book is printed on is certified against the Forest
Stewardship Council® Standards. Griffin Press holds FSC chain
of custody certification SGS-COC-005088. FSC promotes
environmentally responsible, socially beneficial and economically
viable management of the world's forests.

National Library of Australia
Cataloguing-in-Publication data

King, Richard, 1971- author.

On Offence: the politics of indignation / Richard King.

9781922070500 (Australian paperback)
9781922247230 (UK paperback)
9781922072641 (e-book)

1. Respect. 2. Honesty. 3. Offenses against the person. 4. Conduct of life.

179.9

This project has been assisted by
the Australian Government through
the Australia Council, its arts
funding and advisory body.

scribepublications.com.au
scribepublications.co.uk

They came through the border post and found themselves in a grey street: the houses, the curtains at the windows, the clothing worn by Rats and people alike (yes, there were people here, Luka was relieved to see), all grey. The Rats were grey too and the people had acquired a greyish pallor. Overhead, grey clouds allowed a neutral sunlight to filter through. 'They developed a Colour Problem here a little while ago,' Nobodaddy said. 'The Rats who hated the colour yellow because of its, well, cheesiness, were confronted by the Rats who disliked the colour red because of its similarity to blood. In the end all colours, being offensive to someone or other, were banned by the Rathouse — that's the parliament, by the way, although nobody votes for it, it votes for itself, and it basically does what the Over-Rat says.'

— Salman Rushdie, *Luka and the Fire of Life*

For Sarah

Contents

INTRODUCTION

The Mind on Fire

Claim that something is 'offensive', and it is as if the assertion itself has automatically become an argument.

CHRISTOPHER HITCHENS, 'MAU-MAUING THE MOSQUE'

He didn't look like the kind of man who could touch off an international crisis. With his horseshoe moustache and button nose, he looked like Jed Clampett from *The Beverly Hillbillies*, or Yosemite Sam without the hat. Nor was he any great shakes as an orator; to listen to him talk was to conclude pretty quickly that not much was going on behind that tabloid forehead besides an alarming talent for intolerance. Nevertheless, this *Mayflower* nutcase sure kicked up one hell of a stink.

His name was Pastor Terry Jones, and on 12 July 2010 he'd announced his intention to burn the Qur'an, a book he described as 'of the devil'. The burning was scheduled for 11 September, the ninth anniversary of the terrorist attacks on the World Trade Center and the Pentagon. It was now 9 September and Jones was addressing the waiting media outside the Dove World Outreach Center in Florida, where his congregation of around 30 souls had gathered to receive his message of Christian charity. Rolling his hands theatrically, as if displaying fresh stigmata, the pastor declared that the burning was off. God had given him a sign, he said, in the form of an imam who'd agreed to shelve plans for an Islamic centre in downtown New York. Thus Pastor Jones, in climbing down from his threat of libricide, managed to sound even more unhinged than he did when brandishing a box of matches. Well, no matter. Crisis averted. The networks took up their equipment and walked.

The sigh of relief was palpable. In the weeks leading up to 9 September, officials had more or less begged the pastor not to follow through on his threat. The tone was set by General David Petraeus, the commander of US and NATO forces in Afghanistan, who warned that if the burning went ahead it would endanger the lives of US troops. President Obama denounced the plans, describing them as 'a recruitment bonanza' for al-Qaeda and like-minded groups. Leaders from Muslim-majority countries, including Indonesia's Susilo Bambang Yudhoyono, warned the United States of the consequences should the Florida pastor desecrate the Qur'an. Even celebrities chipped in with comments, solicited and duly reported by a media that seems to have decided not only that politics is show business for ugly people, but also that show business is politics for beautiful people. The actress Angelina Jolie was one such. 'I have hardly the words that somebody would do that to somebody's religious book,' Jolie said when asked for her views on the matter.

If the reaction to the threat of the book burning was febrile, the reaction to the reaction was often facile. A few days after the pastor's change of heart, an Australian lawyer named Alex Stewart uploaded a 12-minute video to YouTube in which he tears pages from a Bible and a Qur'an and uses them to make joints. (He later claimed that the smoked substance was not marijuana but grass clippings.) Entitled 'Bible or Koran — which burns best?', the video attracted widespread interest and sparked a number of copycat smokings, as well as solemn denunciations from religious leaders and from Stewart's employers. 'It's just a book,' declares Stewart in the video, still groggy from toking on John 3:15. 'Who cares? It's your beliefs that matter.' Evidently some people cared very much, and they went online to unburden themselves in apoplectic and apocalyptic tones.

This cluster of events and non-events — in which media beat-up met political meltdown, and where the determination to give offence was matched by the determination to take it — did not materialise in a cultural vacuum. On the contrary, bigmouths and bigots were everywhere in the United States in the summer of 2010. The Islamic centre in New York — known originally as Cordoba House, latterly as Park51, and popularly as the 'Ground Zero mosque' — was the focus for much of this demagoguery. Its proposed site was 51 Park Place in Manhattan, just two blocks north of Ground Zero — too close for those (apparently numerous) Americans who were unable to distinguish between ordinary Muslims and Muslims bent on suicide–murder. Too close, certainly, for Newt Gingrich, who compared the plans for Park51 to placing a Nazi sign outside a Holocaust museum, and who suggested, with even greater cretinism, that 'there should be no mosque near Ground Zero in New York so long as there are no churches or synagogues in Saudi Arabia' — a statement that managed to put the United States on the same moral plane as an absolute monarchy in which women can neither drive nor vote. Too close, too, for Sarah Palin, who was moved to send her now infamous tweet urging all moderate Muhammadans to 'pls refudiate' Park51. And too close for Mark Williams of the Tea Party movement, who described the proposed centre as a monument to terrorism.

It wasn't anything of the kind, of course. But canny operators such as Williams know that there's no better way of mobilising support, of drumming up political business, than by stoking popular indignation. And for Americans in search of indignation, 9/11 is often the shortest route. Ground Zero, once a scene of devastation, is now a sort of national sore spot; plans for the site are subject to intense and often acrimonious scrutiny. Even architects elsewhere in the world had better beware if their building designs encroach on the sensitivities of '9/11 families', or those who claim to speak for them. Recently, a Dutch firm felt compelled to apologise when its plans for a pair of skyscrapers in Seoul — joined at the 27th floors by a concrete 'cloud' designed to accommodate restaurants, swimming pools, and gyms — were deemed offensive by furious netizens convinced that the buildings were a visual allusion to the World Trade Center at the moment of immolation.

I've no wish to make light of the feelings about the 9/11 attacks, nor to deny or downplay the seriousness of ceremonial book burning; the symbolic 'killing' of works of literature is a uniquely menacing desecration, redolent of history's darkest periods. But the Sunshine State in 2010 was hardly Berlin in 1933. Neither backed by any government nor endorsed by any party, Terry Jones was a risible figure. The only threat he posed was to sensitivities; the threat of violence came from elsewhere, from those whose sensitivities were in question. And by neglecting to criticise *those* people and mount a defence of freedom of expression, the US government sent a powerful message that the responsibility was all on one side — a message that can only encourage those who would seek to raise a mob in the future, and to raise themselves up in the midst of it. Similarly, the developers of Park51 were mistaken if they thought that by changing its name they could smooth things over with the centre's critics.[1] Those who seek to take offence will always find a reason to do so. Give them an inch and they'll take a foot. Before you know it, you won't have a leg to stand on.

I Feel, Therefore I Am

This book is an attempt to understand the culture of offence-taking and offence-mongering of which this clash of snivelisations is only one example. How did we get to a state in which concepts such as offence and respect are at once so powerful and so hollowed-out that any petty thug or demagogue can attain international notoriety merely by *threatening* to torch a few books? How is it that in New York, of all places — a city in which architectural forms bear witness to successive waves of immigration — cynical politicians with one eye on the polls can pin their colours to a bizarre campaign to prevent the building of a community centre, not on aesthetic or environmental grounds, but because it contains a Muslim 'prayer space' and so might upset the families of those killed on 9/11, an attack carried out 'in the name of Islam'? How, in short, did we arrive at a situation in which the charge of *offence* is so bloody compelling?

Everywhere one looks, offence is being taken — sometimes for good reasons, sometimes for bad ones, but nearly always in a way that implies that offence is something regrettable *in itself*. Respect and offence are fast becoming the 'good cop, bad cop' of a new mood of censoriousness, of self-pity and self-righteousness. Insults are taken for injuries, and hurt feelings are paraded like union banners. Stories of offence or insensitivity are the 21st century's 'marmalade droppers', the scoops that have the news consumer spluttering into his morning coffee.

Andy Warhol got it wrong: it isn't 15 minutes of fame that the man in the street can look forward to, but 15 minutes of infamy.

This new mood of censoriousness goes beyond political correctness. When Prime Minister Kevin Rudd criticised comedian Robin Williams for describing Australians as 'English rednecks', suggesting that Williams might want to spend 'a bit of time in Alabama' before characterising Aussies thus, he was taking umbrage not on behalf of an oppressed minority, but a dynamic democracy with a reputation for plain speaking. Similarly, when Bob Riley, the governor of Alabama, took offence at *Rudd's* remarks, he was responding to a stereotype aimed at the white population of his state and not at its black minority. The language of respect and offence is something more general and less defined than the project to engineer greater equality by avoiding language and habits of mind that tend to entrench discrimination. And while it is often self-satirising (as the Rudd-to-Williams–Riley-to-Rudd squabble demonstrates), it is also very bad for democracy, and for the quality of public debate in general.

What many of these 'controversies' reveal is the willingness of political operators to use offence for their own advantage. The art of taking umbrage has become a must for any politician seeking to win a bit of sympathy and a segment on the evening news. Writing in the online magazine *Slate*, John Dickerson noted in 2008 how indignation had become a major tactic not only in the

US general election but also in the contests leading up to it — campaigns that saw flare-ups over everything from references to Hillary Clinton's cleavage to Barack Obama's African heritage, and in which even tough guy John McCain proved more thin-skinned than a pinot grape.[2] Nor is it only US politicians who seek to use offence in this way. I remember the look of bewilderment — of complete incomprehension — on my friend's face as he sat in his kitchen one Sunday morning poring over the British broadsheets, trying to understand how a political advertising campaign on which he'd worked was being accused of anti-Semitism. The offending poster, which depicted the leader of the Conservative Party, Michael Howard, attempting to hypnotise the electorate with a pocket watch, had been taken by some as an allusion to Fagin, a sly reference to Mr Howard's Romanian-Jewish heritage. Never mind that Dickens' Fagin never hypnotises anyone, or that Howard looks nothing like him, at least as he is popularly imagined. Such objections are a waste of breath when sensitivities are at stake. The o-word does your arguing for you.

This is one of the most worrying aspects of the culture of offence. For what politicians and commentators who push such nonsense seem to look forward to is a general public that is pissed off but ignorant — not an engaged citizenry but an enraged one. Consequently, it is democracy that suffers when sensitivity gains the upper hand. Important questions of who we are and how we should live are lost in the tittle-tattle about who said precisely what about whom, in what tone of voice, and with the use of which epithets. Sometimes whole issues are declared 'no-go' areas; when biologist James Watson made some off-the-cuff remarks about race and intelligence in the middle of a book tour, he caused such a ruckus that the tour was discontinued. But we cannot wish such concerns away, and the more they are ignored the more toxic they become. Though not known for its intellectual rigour, the far right has its philosophical wing, and we had better get our arguments straight if the racist parties of Europe and elsewhere are not to continue their current resurgence. Who would you rather have the discussion about the link between race and intelligence with: the co-discoverer of DNA, or the man with the pit bull and the swastika tattoo?

Clearly, demagoguery is no recent phenomenon; political and religious leaders have always attempted to harness self-pity and resentment in the pursuit of power. But the modern obsession with hurt feelings makes something that was once implicit *explicit*, and in so doing invites us, quite shamelessly, to put our intellects on hold and our feelings on speaker. Having internalised the old slogan of the counterculture, 'the personal is political', we now behave as if the opposite is true, that the political is merely personal. Identifying with causes rather than committing ourselves to them, and mistaking our feelings for political insights, we demand not only the right to take offence but also the right *not to be offended*. Contemporary politics, it sometimes seems, has become an extension of what sociology professor Frank Furedi calls 'therapy culture'; its motto is 'I *feel*, therefore I am.' 'Not in my name!' and 'No blood on my hands!' shrieked the anti-war placards in 2003 — slogans that managed to reduce the decision of whether to go to war in Iraq to an advertisement for *personal* indignation. Thus does feeling take its place at the head of our political priorities.

Technology plays a crucial role in this. While internet and mobile-phone technology has equipped the modern citizen with the tools to challenge the status quo, it has also been the catalyst for the fragmentation and personalisation of political culture in the Western world. The price of technological connection is often political disconnection, as the netizen is apt to respond to the vast, diverse online environment by erecting a wall against the opposition and throwing open the door to like-minded users. Nor is this notion of disconnection merely metaphorical; online communication is no substitute for human contact, and the degeneration of political civility is in many ways the sign and symptom of a world in which human interaction is increasingly mediated by the web. An incautious tweet can cause a storm of protest and, thanks to Twitter, storms of protest are a lot easier to orchestrate than they were in the past.[3] The concept of 'deindividuation' — a loss of inhibition as a result of anonymity — is usually pressed into service by psychologists to explain human behaviour in wartime or riots or other similarly extreme situations.

But with the internet this want of self-control has become a fact of daily life, as shown by the acrimonious comments on articles about everything from politics to celebrity gossip, and by the internet 'trolls' who descend on websites dedicated to people who have died and abuse both the dead and their friends and relatives. Primed as we are to take offence, we grant ourselves leave to dish it out, with the result that online conversations descend all too readily into aggravation and abuse. In the words of Tim Adams of *The Observer*, the internet is creating an 'age of rage'.[4]

Unintended Consequences

Offence, of course, is nothing new. Human beings are social creatures, and the complex interplay of gratitude and vengeance helped us to become the creatures we are. We have evolved to respond quickly to slights and challenges that undermine our status, and to punish those whose behaviour is unhelpful to the interests of the group. But even accepting that *Homo sapiens* is hardwired to take offence, it is clear that the way in which we take offence is a product not just of nature but also of culture, and that the things to which we take offence change according to our time and place.

In Europe in the Middle Ages, by far the worst offences a person of lowly status could commit were against the rich and powerful, if for no other reason than that the rich and powerful had the means to exact revenge. To sin against nobility was to sin against God, since it was He who had set the nobles above us. And, needless to say, to sin against God was to commit the worst offence of all. (In the Christian Bible, the first few commandments — injunctions against the worshiping of false gods, the creation of graven images, and taking the Lord's name in vain — can be roughly translated as 'Respect me or else!')

But as this situation changed, the nature of offence-taking changed as well. Slowly, we moved from a state of affairs in which power and virtue defined civility to one in which consideration for our fellow human beings did.[5] Rights, respect, dignity — these were no longer the preserve of the privileged but the shared inheritance of humankind.

In one sense, what we are witnessing now is a bizarre late phase in this historical process. The rights that we in the West enjoy — the right to vote, the right to a fair trial, the right to freedom of speech and assembly — have done much to alleviate the inequalities that have plagued humanity for most of its history. But rights do not eradicate inequality. In many ways the clamour for 'respect' grows quite naturally from that fact.

Since the 1960s, one major outlet for this clamour has been identity politics, the effect of which has been to give certain attitudes the status of secular heresies. Saying that blacks are inferior to whites or that a woman's place is in the home won't win you many friends down our way, and a good thing too. But the law of unintended consequences is never as conspicuous as when the cause is just, and in the past few years the ironies of history have begun to accumulate at a startling rate. Borrowing from the playbook of 'sensitivity', society's most reactionary elements now demand respect for their feelings. In Europe, demagogic mullahs whip up hatred against a Scandinavian democracy whose newspapers prove insufficiently respectful of their injunctions against depicting the Prophet, while in the United States the spokespeople for a new rightwing populism churn out books with cry-baby titles (*That's No Angry Mob, That's My Mom*; *The Persecution of Sarah Palin*) and accuse Barack Obama of playing the race card. Meanwhile, official censorship hitches a ride on this groaning bandwagon. The UN General Assembly has passed several recent resolutions condemning the 'defamation of religions', and in France it is now a criminal offence to question the genocide of Armenian Turks between 1915 and the early 1920s.

Thus 'sensitivity' nibbles away at the very spirit of free enquiry, without which there would be no formal realm where citizens could question their lot at all.

The Mind on Fire

This book is born of three convictions: that the principle of free speech is meaningless unless it includes the freedom to offend; that the claim to find something hurtful or offensive should be the beginning of the debate, not the end of it; and that the modern fetish for sensitivity is corrosive of genuine civility. Focusing largely on the last 50 years, and on the last two decades in particular, it considers the culture of sensitivity as it plays itself out across the Anglosphere, especially in the countries I feel I know best: the United Kingdom, where I was born; Australia, where I now live; and the United States, of which I've long been a student. Sharing a common language and a common history, the countries of the Anglosphere have tended to follow very similar trajectories when it comes to the politics of indignation. Certainly the US 'culture wars' have their analogues in the United Kingdom and Australia, which share not only a political system but also a political culture. As Rupert Murdoch knows very well, there are differences in what each country will tolerate as regards the nature of public discourse; but that Murdoch can spread his operations across so many continents is itself revealing of a certain amount of common ground.

The Western university is where the story begins, and put forward in the following pages is the tale of a phenomenon that originates there and then moves out into the wider culture, where it takes on a different character according to the country we happen to be talking about. But the similarities are more striking than the differences. The dialectic of political correctness and anti–political correctness is common to all three countries, while the demagoguery of politicians eager to tap into the sensitivities attendant on this clash of perspectives is no respecter of geographical boundaries. Similarly, the confusion between the personal and the political that underlies these phenomena is to be found right across the modern West.

Most importantly, this book argues that the ostentatious taking of offence is very bad for democracy. To proscribe an opinion is to stifle not only the right of a person to express that opinion, but also everyone's right to hear it — a recipe for intellectual laziness, since it is only by engaging with other points of view that we call our own positions into question, refining them when they need refining, and discarding them when they are shown to be flawed. Democracy, I believe, needs a thick skin; though as an Anglo-Saxon living in Australia I've tried to remain cognisant of the fact that this view is rather easier to hold when one's own skin is on the pale side. Nevertheless, I do believe it. To keep the heart on fire and the mind on ice should be the aim of all those who desire social justice.

In the end, the Obama administration's victory over religious pyromania turned out to be a pyrrhic one. On 11 March 2011, Terry Jones burned the Qur'an, after submitting it to a six-hour trial. Subsequently, three UN workers, four Nepalese guards, and five protesters were killed in violence in Afghanistan. President Obama condemned the violence, but others remained unshaken in their view that while to give offence is intolerable, to take it is only natural. 'I don't think we should be blaming any Afghan,' said Staffan de Mistura, the head of the UN Assistance Mission in Afghanistan. 'We should be blaming the person who produced the news — the one who burned the Qur'an.' Even allowing for the fact that de Mistura may have been trying to calm things down, this was a staggering comment to make — one that, in attempting to exonerate the rioters, managed to patronise *all* Afghanis by suggesting that such simple folk could not be held accountable for their actions. Of all the things said in this controversy, this, for me, was the most offensive. *On Offence* is my attempt to say why.

CHAPTER ONE

When Dawkins Met Haggard
a typology of offence

No man lives without jostling and being jostled; in all ways he has to elbow himself through the world, giving and receiving offence.
THOMAS CARLYLE, *SIR WALTER SCOTT*

The evolutionary biologist Professor Richard Dawkins isn't known for his tact and sensitivity. Indeed, in his many dealings with the faithful, the 'evangelical' atheist is usually about as diplomatic as a wolverine with a whisky hangover. But his confrontation with Pastor Ted Haggard of the New Life Church in Colorado Springs was spiky even by his own high standards. No punches were thrown and no furniture was broken, but neither the professor nor the pastor was in the mood to mollify.

The interview was filmed in early 2006 as part of *The Root of All Evil?*, Dawkins' documentary on contemporary religion. The setting was the New Life Church itself, an $18 million 'worship centre' in the foothills of the Rocky Mountains. The centre boasts a 12,000-strong congregation, so to say that Dawkins was behind enemy lines would be to put it mildly. Nevertheless, the professor was determined. After sitting (or squirming) through a noisy service — a lot of arm waving and electric guitars — he set off to meet the big banana himself. Why, he wanted to know, were these born-agains, with their 'childish certainties' and 'Bronze Age myths', as he put it, so intent on attacking science?

'Welcome to the United States!' beamed Pastor Haggard, his arms spread wide. But Dawkins was having none of *that*: 'That was really quite a show you gave us today ... I was almost reminded, if you'll forgive me, of sort of a Nuremberg rally.' Pastor Haggard did forgive him. Laughing off the analogy, he said he preferred to think of it as a 'rock concert'. (Cut to another shot of the service, Haggard moving among his followers as they jumped up and down to unthreatening pop.) Dawkins continued to jab away: wasn't Haggard brainwashing his congregation by insisting that the Bible is the word of God? Not at all, Haggard responded, 'because they don't have to believe that ... [but] the evidence I can present is we've got a book written over 1500 years by 40 different authors on one subject and it doesn't contradict itself'. Though still smiling broadly, Haggard was by now clearly upset by Dawkins' impertinence.

Things began to get really uncomfortable when the conversation turned to 'intelligent design' and the 'evident falsehoods' peddled in its name. Needless to say, this is a subject close to Dawkins' heart, and the spectacle of a 'swaggering' man of God attempting to have his cake and eat it was too much for the staunch Darwinian to stomach. The interview continued, and concluded, like so:

Haggard: We fully embrace the scientific method, as American evangelicals. And we think as time goes along and we discover more and more facts that we'll learn more and more about how God created the heavens and the Earth.

Dawkins: The scientific method clearly demonstrates that the world is four-and-a-half billion years old. Would you accept that?

Haggard: Yeah, you know what you're doing is you are, you're accepting some of the views that are accepted in some portions of the scientific community as fact. Where in fact your grandchildren might listen to the tape of you saying that and laugh at you.

Dawkins: You want to bet?

Haggard: Sometimes it's hard for a human being to study the ear or study the eye and think that happened by accident.

Dawkins: I beg your pardon; did you say by accident? What do you mean by accident?

Haggard: That the eye just formed itself somehow.

Dawkins: Who says it did?

Haggard: Well, some evolutionists say it did.

Dawkins: Not a single one that I've ever met.

Haggard: Really?

Dawkins: Really! You obviously know nothing about the subject of evolution.

Haggard: Or maybe you haven't met the people I have. But you see, you do understand, you do understand, that this issue right here of intellectual arrogance is the reason why people like you have a difficult problem with people of faith. I don't communicate an air of superiority over the people because I know so much more. *[mimicking Dawkins]* And if you only read the books I know, and if you only knew the scientists I knew, then you would be great like me ... Well, sir, there could be many things that you know well. There are other things that you don't know well. As you age, you'll find yourself wrong on some things, right on some other things. But please, in the process of it, don't be arrogant.

For some reason, Dawkins conducted most of the interviews in his documentary while standing, and close-up shots from a handheld camera force the viewer to partake of the queasy atmosphere this creates. But this exchange would make uncomfortable viewing even if the two men had been reclining on chaise longues in cashmere pyjamas and velvet slippers. By the end of the interview, both Dawkins and Haggard were clearly very angry indeed; both had taken offence, and given it.

Lest anyone was left in any doubt about this, the segment ended with a confrontation between Haggard and Dawkins in the church's car park. Dawkins and his crew were packing up to leave when Haggard arrived in a utility truck and instructed them to remove themselves from his property upon pain of another interview — with Colorado's boys in blue. We cannot hear this altercation, but according to Professor Dawkins, '[Haggard] then said a very curious thing. He said, "You called my children animals."' In a piece to camera, the biologist speculated that this was a reference to his defence of Darwinian evolution: 'He thought I was saying that his flock were animals,' said Dawkins, before adding, 'which in a sense I was.'

Going Ape

The Dawkins–Haggard argument will not go down in the annals of history as one of the most spectacular instances of offence-taking. The Rushdie affair and the Danish cartoons crisis probably beat it for political import, while for simple entertainment value William F. Buckley threatening to punch Gore Vidal in the mouth for calling him a 'pro-crypto-Nazi' puts it firmly in the shade. But the more I thought about this disagreement, the more I came to discern in it a sort of typology of indignation. The confrontation at the New Life Church is not an event of great consequence. But for the student of offendedness, it serves as an excellent point of departure.

Take, to begin with, Dawkins' words to camera: 'He thought I was saying that his flock were animals, which in a sense I was.' Dawkins is right, of course; human beings *are* animals, and we have evolved over thousands of years. Moreover, according to the Darwinian theory of which Dawkins is such a ferocious advocate, our behaviour is shaped by our evolutionary past. So does it not make sense to enquire into the role *offence* might have played in the evolution of the human species? To put it another way: to what extent were the feelings of offence on show in Colorado 'selected for'?

To an extent, the answer to that question depends on what we think human beings are. The English philosopher Thomas Hobbes took the view that social life did not come naturally to the human species. Life in a state of nature, he wrote, was 'solitary, poor, nasty, brutish, and short'. The French philosopher Jean-Jacques Rousseau disagreed with Hobbes about the brutishness, but still thought that humans were naturally solitary. Both saw society as something artificial, imposed from without. But according to evolutionary science, humans are not naturally solitary. On the contrary, we are fundamentally social. As the primatologist Frans de Waal puts it in *Primates and Philosophers*: '[D]escended from highly social ancestors — a long line of monkeys and apes — we have been group-living forever ... Any zoologist would classify our species as *obligatorily gregarious*.'[1]

That human beings are social animals is uncontroversial, at least in the scientific community. But there are key questions about the extent to which, or in what ways, our minds are shaped by evolution. In particular, there is widespread disagreement about whether morality is a natural phenomenon. Is morality something 'painted on', or do we come equipped with it? Advocates for the first position include 'Darwin's bulldog' Thomas Huxley, whom de Waal identifies as the founder of 'veneer theory' — the notion of morality as a 'cultural overlay'. But others, including de Waal himself, reject this view of morality. For them, the 'moral emotions' emerge from the fact that we are social creatures. Our instinctive feelings of right and wrong, these advocates of natural morality suggest, are intimately mapped into our evolutionary past. De Waal invites us to think of ourselves not as solid clay garden gnomes to which a coating of moral paint has been applied, but as Russian dolls whose outer morality is fundamentally related to a series of inner 'pre-human' selves. 'If we are indeed born competitors,' he writes, 'how did we decide to transform ourselves into model citizens? Can people for generations maintain behaviour that is out of character, like a shoal of piranhas that decides to turn vegetarian?'[2]

De Waal is certainly not the first to worry about this 'curious dualism'. The Scottish philosopher Adam Smith mooted the idea of an inborn moral sense as early as 1759. In *The Theory of Moral Sentiments*, Smith wrote of human beings' 'fellow-feeling' and suggested that our natural empathy with others underlies our first moral judgments: 'Nature, when she formed man for society, endowed him with an original desire to please, and an original aversion to offend his brethren.'[3] Darwin, who was influenced by Smith's work, took a similar view. In opposition to Huxley (who on this question, at least, refused to come to heel), he wrote, 'the social instincts, which no doubt were acquired by man, as by the lower animals, for the good of the community, will from the first have given to him some wish to aid his fellows, and some feeling of sympathy'.[4] In this view, we have not gone from being amoral animals to moral human beings. Rather, we have gone from being social animals to (sorry, Ted) *moral animals*.[5]

According to the anthropologist Christopher Boehm, we have to go back a quarter of a million years in order to understand the evolution of morality. Around that time, Boehm suggests, collaborative hunting of large animals became more productive than solo hunting. But such collaboration could only work if the profits were shared among all the hunters. Thus we moved, in Boehm's view, from a system that was essentially hierarchical to one that was 'devoutly egalitarian'.[6] Early humans who were skilled at cooperating would have fared better than ones who weren't, as would those who had the 'fittest' sharing rules. Those who hung back or ate more than their fair share would have been shunned by the group, or worse. Boehm shows how contemporary hunter-gatherers use strict social rules to suppress 'free riding'. But his principal point is that, over millennia, these rules have become internalised. Our feelings about what is fair and unfair are written down in our DNA.

In one sense, this seems counterintuitive. After all, Dawkins himself uses the phrase 'the selfish gene' to describe the way in which natural selection operates. But as he points out in his bestselling book *The God Delusion*, it's the *gene* that's selfish, not the organism. Genes can ensure their own 'selfish' survival by engendering altruism in their hosts. As Dawkins puts it:

> Natural selection favours genes that predispose individuals, in relationships of asymmetric need and opportunity, to give when they can, and to solicit giving when they can't. It also favours tendencies to remember obligations, bear grudges, police exchange relationships and punish cheats who take, but don't give when their turn comes.[7]

Our natural sociability gives rise to the need for reciprocity, which in turn gives rise to the sense of unfairness. And that, of course, is where offence comes in.

This is not to say that offence is a strictly 'moral' response. The Finnish philosopher Edvard Westermarck drew a distinction between emotions such as resentment, which depend on our feelings about how we ought to be treated, and more detached 'moral emotions', such as sympathy with another victim of injustice.[8] Offence in its most basic form is an emotion of the first sort; it is instinctive and immediate. 'We should resent more from a sense of the propriety of resentment,' wrote Adam Smith in *The Theory of Moral Sentiments*, 'than because we feel in ourselves the furies of that disagreeable passion.'[9] But this is easier said than done. Feelings of offence are not optional; they arrive unbidden, and can take us by surprise. And sometimes they can have devastating consequences.

'The dark side of the sense of fairness is the sense of unfairness, which results in gloating when you've got away with being unfair, or else guilt; and in rage and vengeance, when the unfairness has been visited upon you.' So writes Margaret Atwood in *Payback*, her absorbing little book on debt, before noting that children begin saying 'That's not fair!' around the age of four.[10] At that age, of course, human beings do not possess a sophisticated system of morality. But what they do seem to have is a rough sense of justice, so that when the villain in a fairytale, say, receives his comeuppance they are filled with satisfaction. We may imagine that the stories we tell our children are teaching them to think or behave morally. But to some extent we are merely pandering to a sense of fairness already in place.

Just how powerful this sense of fairness is can be demonstrated scientifically. The psychologist Leda Cosmides has shown how experimental subjects are better able to solve complex puzzles when those puzzles are framed in human terms, especially when the point of the puzzle is to figure out when someone is behaving dishonestly or selfishly in a social exchange — a finding that suggests that our sense of fairness is a cognitive as well as an emotional phenomenon.[11] Or take the Ultimatum Game. In this classic economic experiment, Player A is given 20 $1 notes and told that if he wants to keep any of the money he must share the notes with Player B. If Player B accepts his offer, both get to keep the money they've agreed upon. However, if Player B rejects A's offer, neither player gets to keep any of the money. Cold logic predicts that Player A will offer Player B one $1 note (the lowest offer allowed under the rules) and that Player B will accept the offer, since even one dollar is better than nothing. But this isn't what happens. In nearly 50 per cent of cases, Player A offers to split the money with Player B — an offer that Player B is happy to accept. Most Player Bs are also happy to accept $9 or $8, but when Player A's offer drops to $7, around half of the Player Bs reject it, thus depriving both players of any money at all. The effect of the study is to show how rationality is subservient to more powerful drives, and how finely tuned our ability is to detect those who 'cheat' in social situations.[12]

When such social cheating occurs, our natural response is to feel offended. But it isn't only non-reciprocal behaviour that causes people to take offence. Just as powerful is the sense that someone has shown a lack of respect. Statistics show that many murders occur between acquaintances, often as the result of a minor insult,[13] while in the United States an entire violent culture has built up around the notion of 'respect'. Needless to say, this violent culture is a social problem first: lack of opportunity and poor social conditions have created a situation in America's inner cities in which drug-related gun crime is rife. Even minor insults can have fatal consequences when a person's standing in the community depends solely on his reputation for toughness. Nevertheless, the feelings of offence that lead to such consequences are often genuine. Disrespect is a powerful incitement.

Some interesting thoughts on this topic can be found on the website *Less Wrong*, 'a community blog devoted to refining the art of human rationality'. In 2009, in a discussion about social status, one commenter suggested that high social status was good for men because it allowed them to have sex with lots of 'extremely attractive women'. Several other commenters objected to this suggestion, which prompted a regular contributor to try to identify what it was about the comment that made it so offensive to others. From the comments of those who took offence, the contributor identified three main objections: 'to be thought of, talked about as, or treated like a non-person; analysis of behaviour that puts the reader in the group being analysed, and the speaker outside it; [and] exclusion from the intended audience'. The thing that links these three objections, the contributor suggested, is *status* — the very topic under discussion when the offending comment was made.[14] In seeming to treat women as sex objects rather than as equal human beings, and in addressing the *Less Wrong* community in a way that seemed to exclude women from the discussion, the commenter had undermined women's status, and other commenters had responded accordingly.

Clearly, the Dawkins–Haggard spat had a lot to do with status and reputation. As Dawkins suggests in his voiceover, Haggard is 'a powerful man' with a 'hotline to God, and to George Bush'. To some extent, Dawkins 'drew the foul' by choosing to confront him on his home ground, and by doing so in such a hostile manner. Similarly, by suggesting that Dawkins' opinions were of no more consequence than anyone else's, Haggard effectively cocked a snook not only at his interviewer but also at his field of expertise. That the interview was set up to make the interviewee uncomfortable added yet more gunpowder to the mix. At times in the discussion it looks as if Haggard is about to hit Dawkins, who looks both angry and anxious. The discussion is conducted at an intellectual level that would be entirely beyond a human being living, say, 10,000 years ago, but the body language and facial expressions of the two adult males conducting it would, I imagine, be completely familiar.

Religion and its Discontents

But what of the *substance* of that discussion? So far, we've considered human nature as a factor in the taking of offence. Yet the ideas under discussion are no less important. Dawkins and Haggard were not discussing whether cricket is a superior game to baseball, or whether The Beatles made better records than Elvis. They were discussing the most important question of all time: is the universe a divine creation? Haggard says it is. Dawkins says it isn't, or that no evidence has come forward to say it is. Strictly speaking, I'm agnostic on the issue (though a lot closer to Dawkins' view than to Haggard's). But of one thing I'm absolutely sure: more offence has been taken over this question than any other in the history of humankind.

Not that religious sentiment is necessarily confined to the realm of ideas. According to many scientists, religion could well be a natural phenomenon, building on pre-existing patterns, or psychological rules of thumb. Take the phenomenon of reciprocal behaviour we examined earlier. Many religions and systems of ethics give a central place to reciprocity. 'Whatsoever thou wouldst that men should not do to thee,' said the ancient Jewish sage Hillel the Elder, 'do not do that to them. This is the whole Law.' Similarly, Jesus, in the Sermon on the Mount, handed down the 'golden rule': 'Do unto others as you would have them do unto you.' And Confucius, when asked if there was just one word that could serve as a guide to the moral life, suggested the word *shu* — reciprocity. In this sense, at least, there is no rigid distinction between the scientific view of human nature and the religious one. The US psychologist Jonathan Haidt even goes so far as to suggest that evolution may have favoured religious societies; gods, he writes, are 'commitment devices' that enhance 'cooperation, trust, and mutual aid'.[15] Certainly, the idea that religion performs a binding function has an impressive pedigree. For the great sociologist Émile Durkheim, it was from religion that humanity derived its strongest sense of collective consciousness.[16]

This happy picture is all very well, but religion is coercive as well as cohesive. Indeed, it is cohesive *because* it is coercive, a point made succinctly by H. L. Mencken: 'People say we need religion when what they really mean is we need police.'[17] Moreover, religions are at their most coercive not when someone has shown a lack of reciprocity, but when someone has committed heresy or blasphemy (or, in certain religions, apostasy). The philosopher Thomas Aquinas considered blasphemy to be worse than murder, while respect for the Big Man gets a lot more attention in the Ten Commandments than respect for one's neighbour. And, since mankind is made in God's image, the faithful are often extremely touchy about anything that reminds them of our closeness to nature. Sex, of course, is a big worry, as is the theory of evolution.

While Durkheim was no doubt right to say that religion served a cohesive function in the past, in the modern world the picture is more complicated. To some extent, the very thing that made religion useful to primitive societies makes it unsuited to modern ones. Not only are there conflicts *between* religions — as in the case of Israel, where any hope of a two-state solution is poisoned by Orthodox Jews on the one hand and Islamic fundamentalists on the other — but there are also frequent conflicts *within* them: between Sunni and Shia Islam, for example, or Catholic and Protestant Christianity. Nor is this a new phenomenon. Such was the antipathy between different sects in the early days of Christianity that their members would often separate to different parts of the amphitheatre in order not to be eaten by the same animals.[18] When it comes to religion, more often than not one's company and two's a crowd.

The reason for this is so obvious it is very often missed. The notion of revealed truth *necessarily* entrains intolerance. Religion, as the late Christopher Hitchens pointed out, is not just the claim to know that God exists; it is also the claim *to know his mind* — to know what He wants you to eat on a Friday, to know with whom and in what ways He permits you to have sexual intercourse, to know how many times a day and in what direction He expects you to pray.[19] Those who put their faith in holy books are always prone to intolerance for the simple reason that holy books purport to be the word of God. In a sense, it is the believer's *duty* to take offence when that word is denied, whether by members of another religion or by people with no religion at all.

Needless to say, that second group is the one with which Professor Dawkins is in sympathy, and I don't think it's being melodramatic to suggest that his anger contains an echo of the millions to have suffered at the hands of the religious. The criticism of religion, Karl Marx suggested, is the foundation of intellectual life, and such progress as modern humans have made has often been made in the teeth of faith. Until very recently in human history, free thought was antithetical to religion, and in many parts of the world it still is. The word 'philosophy' means 'love of wisdom'. But how can an individual reconcile the love of wisdom with unconditional faith in God? Many are the philosophers — from Socrates to Giordano Bruno to Tommaso Campanella to Baruch Spinoza — who know the answer to that question: he can't.

Socrates was condemned to death for calling into question the gods of the state, and his trial and execution are potent reminders that the freedom to speak and to exercise one's conscience is the precondition for philosophy's existence. Partly for this reason, freedom of speech has inspired some of the most passionate works of the mind. John Milton's *Areopagitica* (1644) and John Stuart Mill's *On Liberty* (1859) both deal with this most fundamental of questions, and make roughly similar points: that to ban an opinion is to ban not only the right of a person to express that opinion, but also everyone's right to hear it; and that to abolish certain points of view is to invite intellectual idleness. The contemporary philosopher A. C. Grayling says that the right to freedom of speech is the most important right of all — because without it, it is simply impossible to subject all our other rights to scrutiny.[20] The view is traceable to Socrates, whose dialogic method was designed to show how the clash of radically different viewpoints could be harnessed in the service of truth. Socrates and Grayling are separated by two-and-a-half millennia, but on one point they would agree entirely: the 'heretic' may be right and received opinion wrong.

As Grayling suggests in *Towards the Light*, the story of the struggle for liberty and rights is the story of a chain reaction. The clamour for religious liberty that grew out of the Spanish Inquisition and the countless horrors perpetrated in its name led eventually to the Protestant Reformation, which, though it spawned its own atrocities, contained the seeds of a revolution 'aiming for liberty in the kingdom of the mind'. From this flowed the erosion of the idea of heresy, a burgeoning spirit of free enquiry (which further undermined the claims of religion), and the crucial attempt to extend that spirit to every area of human endeavour: that is to say, the Enlightenment. And from that emerged the worldview Dawkins represents. The story of modern science, writes Grayling, 'is also the story of the struggle by religious orthodoxy to retain control over how the universe is to be seen, and where the limits of legitimate enquiry lie. To make science possible, religion's claim to hegemony over the mind had to be broken.'[21] No wonder the professor and the pastor didn't exactly hit it off.

Intimate Diversity

As societies become gradually less religious, their notions of civility change. In *Civility: a cultural history*, Benet Davetian suggests the West has gone from a situation in which *virtue* defines civility to one in which *consideration* for one's fellow human beings does so. This change, he suggests, came as a result of increased self-awareness during the Renaissance. As people became more individualistic, they also developed an increased awareness of the effects of their actions upon other people. Of course, the one form of civility did not entirely displace the other, and we find no shortage of conflict between the two in the centuries leading up to our own. In the 19th century, this conflict was discernible in the tension between morality and manners. Davetian notes how evangelical moralists considered 'manners on their own … the stuff of corruption and hypocrisy'.[22]

Clearly, the argument between Dawkins and Haggard was not a disagreement of that sort. But it was, to some extent, a cultural clash. As anyone who has travelled overseas will know, civility codes and etiquette conventions vary radically from culture to culture. Even countries that have a lot in common differ in point of decorum and manners. To a large degree, the US Constitution draws on British traditions of liberty, but in other ways the younger country defines itself *against* the older one. In the early days of the Republic, for example, Thomas Jefferson sought to cultivate an anti-aristocratic civility that would cut through all the English guff about heredity and proper breeding and release instead 'the natural gentleman'.[23] Less class-bound than their British cousins, Americans favour directness and ease, and I don't think it's drawing too long a bow to suggest that when Haggard talks of Dawkins' 'air of superiority', he's reacting at some level to being told his business by a rather stuffy-sounding Englishman.

One of the stranger books on my shelves is *The Book of Etiquette* by Lady Troubridge. Published in 1926, this tome contains all the advice you will ever need on how to dress for evening parties, engaging a servant, or writing a letter. But Lady T. is not content to set out the rules of acceptable conduct. She would also like us to understand the context in which such rules emerged. Here she is on 'the need for etiquette':

One of the first necessities of the savage was to devise some means of showing savages of other tribes that he did not wish to fight — that he wanted to live in peace. At first it was difficult to do this, for primeval man was suspicious: he was forced to be so, for his life depended on his acuteness. Slowly, however, certain signs and observances were established, and savages began to understand them as greetings of peace and goodwill. The salutation of today is a direct result of this early necessity.[24]

There is more than a kernel of truth in this. The need for manners *is* related to a desire to avoid unnecessary conflict. But there is something rather absurd about a member of the English aristocracy suggesting that etiquette solves societal antagonisms. Etiquette conventions, as often as not, are inclusive precisely because they are *exclusive*. They serve to *reinforce* status differences, not to undermine them in some spirit of equality. Sometimes this self-separation is explicit, as in the attempt in 1950s Britain to delineate upper-class and middle-class (or U and non-U) sociolects — a project memorialised in John Betjeman's poem 'How to Get On in Society', in which a middle-class hostess betrays her origins by using words such as 'toilet' (instead of 'lavatory') and 'serviette' (instead of 'napkin'). Sometimes it is more unconscious, as when Lady Troubridge lays down the law on the proper way to pronounce Pierrepont, Ponsonby, Pontefract, Pugh, Pytchley, and other names 'in common usage'.[25] In either case, the effect is the same: to draw a thick black line between the haves and the chavs.

When it comes to differences of nationality and ethnicity, civility codes play an even bigger role. In a talk delivered at the Oxford Union, the British musician Gerard Hoffnung drew an enormous roar of laughter from the audience when he suggested that as a tourist guide he had instructed foreign visitors to 'shake hands with all the passengers' upon entering a British Rail compartment. To anyone familiar with British reticence, the suggestion is ridiculous; but in a sense this kind of thing happens all the time, and not always with such amusing consequences. To talk too loudly can cause offence in some cultures, while to talk too quietly can cause offence in others. The same is true of exuberant hand gestures, and a range of other behaviours. Hence the imperative attributed to Saint Ambrose — 'When in Rome, do as the Romans do' — is surely the best travel advice ever given, with the possible exception of 'Don't drink the water'.

But of course not everyone who comes into contact with a person from a different culture is a traveller. The modern city, more often than not, is one in which different cultures mix. Urban centres such as London and New York are filled with people from diverse backgrounds, and this diversity can sometimes foster a certain amount of suspicion between communities. Deploying paradox as only he could, G. K. Chesterton made a related point when he wrote that the 20th-century city was in many ways a narrower place than the small village of times gone by because in the latter environment one was on intimate terms with one's neighbours. Consequently, he suggested, the village-dweller knew more about humanity in general than his alienated city cousin.[26] While Chesterton overstated the case, his underlying point is sound. Just because an environment is diverse, it doesn't mean that everyone in it values that diversity.

This point is so central to the subject of offence that it is difficult to overestimate. Evolved to live in small communities, *Homo sapiens* is now at large in a new and alien environment — one replete with opportunities to give and take offence. Moreover, modern communications technology has created a world in which it is increasingly difficult to avoid opinions, or language or humour, that may not be to one's own taste. 'We are all neighbours now,' writes Timothy Garton Ash, in an article delineating the threats to free speech that emerge as a result of this 'new intimacy of diversity'.[27] We sure are, but we aren't always neighbourly.

Consider, for example, the countless battles that have been fought over blasphemous or obscene language since television became a fact of life. Swearing, as Steven Pinker has shown in his indispensable book *The Stuff of Thought*, is a naturally evolved phenomenon by which the speaker effectively forces the listener to have an unpleasant or emotionally charged thought. (The production and perception of taboo words, he suggests, are the preserve of the ancient parts of the brain that deal with negative emotions such as disgust.) There are many different types of swearing, and many reasons why we swear. For example, we swear to express strong emotion ('So, you've been fucking your secretary') and to intimidate adversaries ('Go fuck yourself'); we also swear for emphasis ('This is some cool shit') and to convey informality ('Same old shit, different day').[28] As Pinker suggests, these forms of swearing are all appropriate to their separate contexts. But in the age of television and the internet, such contextual swearing is available to all, even to those who don't want to hear it. Consequently, people can be offended by swearing even when it is idiomatic. Language that may be benign in one situation can become malignant in a different one.

This holds true for humour, too. Like swearing, humour is a natural phenomenon — one that many commentators regard as essential to human creativity.[29] For example, Professor Peter McGraw has argued that jokes are 'benign violations' — that laughter and amusement result when normality is disrupted in a non-threatening way. The origins of humour, McGraw suggests, may lie in our evolutionary past. Organisms that could separate benign violations from real threats would have benefited greatly, and laughter itself may have evolved from the noises we made to signal false alarms; that a movement in the bushes, say, was young Ug coming back from a hunting expedition and not a sabre-toothed tiger with cubs to feed.[30] True or not, it is certainly the case that while a joke may put certain people at their ease, it can make others uncomfortable, and that modern communication technologies make such conflicting responses inevitable; a joke in the wrong company may cause offence, and in the plugged-in, logged-on 21st century the wrong company is never far away. Some jokes may be benign violations in certain contexts and merely violations in others. 'In the Garden of Eden Lay Adam' may set the table on a roar in New College; but in the New Life Church in Colorado, it's apt to earn you a slap round the chops.

Don't Be Arrogant

The varieties of indignation we've explored in this chapter — natural, philosophical, and cultural — all, I'm sure, had their part to play in the confrontation between Dawkins and Haggard. But there is one form of offence-taking I haven't mentioned. A relatively recent phenomenon, and ubiquitous in contemporary debates about politics, religion, and much else besides, it can perhaps be usefully described as the *how-dare-you-question-my-beliefs* response. It is not the offence over anything in particular, but the feeling that a person should be *free* from offence — the belief that one's beliefs should be immune from criticism.

You can hear it in Haggard's animadversions about Dawkins' 'intellectual arrogance'. By this stage the pastor's blood is up, but it is significant that he chooses to express his irritation in these terms. In the past, a man in Haggard's position would have fallen back on professions of faith and exhortations about the one true path. But Haggard's response is more self-pitying than self-righteous. It's not the fact that Dawkins doesn't believe in God that upsets him; it's the fact that he thinks, or appears to think, that his beliefs are *superior* to Haggard's. Never mind that *anyone* who takes a view on *anything* necessarily considers that view superior to the other views that could have been adopted. In the touchy 21st century, where belief plays second fiddle to feeling, such points are lost, or else put aside in the search for intellectual self-esteem. 'There could be many things you know well,' Haggard informs his interviewer in a tone of icy magnanimity; 'but please … don't be arrogant'.

Arrogant? Haggard has just spent an entire morning strutting up and down in front of thousands of people, enjoining them to worship an invisible deity whose wishes and plans for humanity he considers himself qualified to elucidate. Really, what is more arrogant: to claim that the universe is made with *me* in mind and that only by listening to what *I* have to say are you guaranteed a stint in the afterlife; or to call these beliefs into question? '[W]hy beholdest thou the mote that is in thy brother's eye,' runs Matthew 7:3, 'but considerest not the beam that is in thine own eye?' The pastor demands humility from his interviewer, but his own lack of humility is scarcely less conspicuous.

Nor is Haggard the only holy man to adopt the role of injured party. In 2010, the Pope's personal preacher, Father Raniero Cantalamessa, caused a storm of protest when he appeared to suggest that the criticism levelled at the Catholic Church over its handling of various child-rape cases was reminiscent of anti-Semitism. Even if we overlook the fact that the Catholic Church was, ahem, *more sympathetic than it might have been* to the far-right movements of the 20th century, and that its holy book, in convicting the Jews, born and unborn, of the unique crime of deicide, contains the original warrant for anti-Semitism, this analogy would still be inappropriate. Rich in both treasure and influence, the Catholic Church is scarcely less powerful in the early 21st century than it was in the time of Torquemada. To cast itself in the role of victim when what is at stake is the victimisation of boys and girls in its charge is worse than absurd; it is obscene. But that is the situation today — a situation in which even the powerful find it expedient to parade their hurt feelings.

The problem is not the hurt feelings themselves; the problem is the belief that hurt feelings should take priority over argument. The word *offend* derives from *offendere*, a Latin word meaning 'to strike against'. But in the 21st century, it isn't only offence, but also the *taking* of offence, that is weaponised — that is used to strike against intellectual opponents. Though this is not a new phenomenon, it is certainly newly prominent. And for anyone who cares about the world of ideas, it should be a cause of deep concern.

CHAPTER TWO

———————

From Enlightenment to Entitlement

Now, I'm all for verbal uplift. I like being called Ms. I don't want
people saying 'man' when they mean me, too. I'm willing to make
an issue of these things. But I know that even when all women are
Ms, we'll still get sixty-five cents for every dollar earned by a man.
Minorities by any other name — people of colour or whatever —
will still bear a huge burden of poverty, discrimination, and racial
harassment. Verbal uplift is not the revolution.

BARBARA EHRENREICH, 'THE CHALLENGE FOR THE LEFT'

It was an inspired piece of political branding, all the more
impressive for the fact that the organisation from which it
sprang regarded branding as part of the problem. On 13
July 2011, the anti-consumerist magazine *Adbusters* posted
the following message on its website:

#OCCUPYWALLSTREET

Are you ready for a Tahrir moment? On Sept 17, flood
into lower Manhattan, set up tents, kitchens, peaceful
barricades and occupy Wall Street.

The 'Tahrir moment' was a reference to Cairo's Tahrir Square, where pro-democracy demonstrators had gathered a few months before, at the height of the Arab Spring. *Adbusters* envisaged a similar gathering, the principal objective of which would be to protest against the influence of money — specifically, corporate money — on US politics. The financial crisis of 2008 was, they reasoned, born of the relationship between money and power — between capital and the Capitol — and the subsequent government bailout of the banks an instance of what Gore Vidal once described as socialism for the rich and free enterprise for the poor. It was time for the people to make a stand.

And make a stand they did. On the afternoon of 17 September, as per the Canadian magazine's instructions, a crowd of around 1000 protesters marched through New York's financial district. The chants were unambiguous: 'Wall Street is our street' and 'Power to the people, not to the banks.' That night, the 'occupation' began. Despite resistance from the NYPD, an estimated 300 protesters spent the night in Zuccotti Park. Over the next few weeks, that number would swell, as the movement grew to encompass unions and all manner of political pressure groups, as well as many non-affiliated citizens — all of them marching under the ingenious slogan 'We are the 99%'.

That, too, was a clever piece of branding, one that spoke to the way in which the world appeared to be moving in precisely the direction prophesied by Karl Marx in *The Communist Manifesto*: towards a state of affairs in which wealth and power (which for Marx came to more or less the same thing) are massively concentrated in the hands of a few, and in which the vast majority of humans live in a state of economic uncertainty. In a country where the two major political parties were funded by big corporations, that was an impressive spectacle, and few were the genuine social democrats who dismissed the Occupy movement out of hand. These were not the usual suspects. Inscribed in the idea of the 99 per cent were the stirrings of a new political consciousness.

The problem was that this broadness of base tended to translate into a vagueness of message. Notwithstanding the disagreements between various factions in the Arab Spring, the Tahrir Square protesters knew exactly what they wanted — an end to the Hosni Mubarak regime, followed by free and fair elections. Similarly, the anti-austerity protesters in Spain (and other European countries) whose example inspired the Occupy protest were much clearer than their American comrades when it came to articulating their demands. In fact, the Occupy protesters didn't have any demands as such — just a few rather fuzzy principles. Even *Adbusters'* original idea to demand a presidential commission into the influence of money on US politics was dropped at an early general assembly (a nightly meeting where protesters could have their say about the movement or about the running of the Zuccotti Park encampment), presumably because the demonstrators were wary of being dictated to. Eschewing vertical decision-making, the organisers of the Occupy movement exhibited an attachment to participatory democracy that bordered on the fanatical. Indeed, they put participation ahead of a clear political agenda. Everyone knew what Occupy stood for, but no one seemed to know what it wanted.

Of course, some members of the movement may argue that I've missed the point — that the Occupy protest was more concerned to put forward a model for change than a program for it; that it was not a traditional protest movement but a miracle of self-assembly and organisation. They would have a case: improvised facilities such as 'the people's library', a public library set up in Zuccotti Park, were a tribute to the demonstrators' solidarity, while the 'people's mic' and the silent hand gestures adopted in the general assemblies showed the kind of cooperation and ingenuity without which real change would be impossible.[1] To that extent, the medium was the message. But without a central demand or focus, the idea of the 99% lacked any unifying power. Consequently, a different kind of politics — one based not on solidarity but on difference — quickly began to assert itself.

That kind of politics was most conspicuously manifest in the People of Color (POC) working group, which was set up at the beginning of October 2011 and sought to 'ensure equitable involvement of all marginalised groups, and a racial justice lens that also takes into account other aspects of identities (such as gender, class, sexuality, religion, language, nationality, and ability)'.[2] Often referred to as

POCcupy, the POC was (legitimately) concerned with the paucity of African Americans and other minorities within the Occupy movement. And yet its efforts were not all, or even principally, in the direction of wider and more diverse recruitment; on the contrary, the POC would often talk as if the whole idea of the 99 per cent was suspect. 'The POC's purpose is to keep the movement accountable,' one of its leaders is quoted as saying, 'to keep these progressive white activists accountable.'[3] It established 'oppression workshops' for those who took part in Occupy meetings — meetings in which the speakers were 'majority white and male, which is the highest privilege you can have in this social construct that is our society'.[4] Since roughly half of Americans are female, and a significant minority of them non-white, the effect of such statements was to call into question the coherence of Occupy's central slogan. 'We are the 99%' made sense if the principal target was plutocracy, but not if the principal target was prejudice.

Clearly, POCcupy had a point. Black Americans and other minorities had suffered disadvantage, economic and otherwise, for generations, and little had been done about it. If white Americans were now feeling the pinch, it was important for them to remember what minority Americans had suffered and were suffering, and the POC made sure that they did. Nevertheless, if 'the 99%' was to be worth more than the pizza boxes it was scrawled on, it meant stressing unity in the face of wealth inequality — and believing that greater wealth equality would mean a fairer society for *all* Americans, of whatever colour, sex, or persuasion.

It was not to be. As the novelty of the Occupy protest wore off and the euphoria of its early days receded, its atmosphere grew increasingly discordant. Different constituencies pushed their own causes. Some feminists claimed that since Wall Street was a symbol of the much larger problem of patriarchal power, any movement that failed to put women and women's rights at the top of its agenda was not just irrelevant but part of the problem.[5] Meanwhile, some Native American protesters left the demonstration, claiming to feel unrepresented by it and suggesting that as their land had been 'occupied' since the arrival of the Pilgrim Fathers, the language of the movement was inappropriate. The organisers of some general assemblies attempted to manage such sensitivities with a system called the 'progressive stack': a mild, if telling, form of affirmative action designed to give disadvantaged groups more chances to speak. Nevertheless, many general assemblies descended into abuse and fistfights. In the winter of 2011, according to a CBS news report, tensions were especially marked: 'Protesters accused each other of being patriarchal and racist and domineering. Nobody could agree on anything and nobody was in charge. The moderators went on strike and refused to show up, followed in quick succession by the people who kept the meeting minutes.'[6] Nor is this merely the characterisation of a major television network in thrall to a 'corporate' view of the Occupy movement. Writing in the leftwing webzine *CounterPunch*, the late economics professor Thomas Naylor expressed similar concerns:

> Some General Assemblies have a distinct touchy-feely character in which process always trumps substantive discussion … Mutuality, inclusiveness, and political correctness are far more important than political strategy. Hurt feelings are to be avoided at all cost.[7]

In short, a protest that began as an attempt to redefine and re-energise leftwing politics was more hampered than helped by a political outlook, and a set of political priorities, associated with an older form of activism. Those priorities were based on real concerns; but the terms in which they tended to be articulated served to undermine the Occupy movement, at least as it was originally conceived. As such, they provide a kind of allegory of leftwing politics in the last 30 years. The protest inspired by *los indignados* of the Spanish anti-austerity movement fell foul of a different species of indignation, the history and peculiar character of which necessarily provides the starting point for any analysis of the politics of offence in the late 20th and early 21st century.

Clumsy Justice

The term 'political correctness' has a period feel; like shoulder-pads and Filofaxes, it seems to belong to an earlier epoch. And yet the habits of mind and ideological assumptions associated with it continue to exert a powerful influence. The reflexive register of 'sensitivity'; the too-easy accusation of 'disrespect' levelled at political opponents; the rise of politics as a form of therapy; and the way in which these trends come together to undermine authentic civility: the roots of these phenomena are deep and tangled. But one major source of nourishment is that combination of anti-elitist rhetoric and ideological conformity once described as 'the dictatorship of virtue'.

But first, what *is* political correctness? The question is more complex than it seems, partly because the term itself has become a kind of political swearword, a bat with which to belabour the left whenever it sticks up for ethnic minorities or other disadvantaged groups. Some even make the case that PC is an 'engineered' term: a bit of conservative heavy artillery to be wheeled out when the enemy appears on the horizon. Certainly, it only came to prominence in the culture wars of the 1980s, when it was more often on the lips of conservatives than on those of liberals and leftwingers. Nevertheless, I don't think it's accurate to define political correctness in this way. For one thing, the term was certainly current on the left in the 1970s, though it was often deployed ironically, in a way that pointed to the tendency towards ideological line-toeing on the hard left in particular. For another, it is clear that 'political correctness' does describe a real phenomenon, even if one often distorted or exaggerated by conservative ideologues. Or rather, it describes two related phenomena.

The first is an often obsessive interest in the *power* of language: an awareness of, and sensitivity to, the way in which language carries political meanings of which the speaker may be unaware.[8] And the second is a more general critical approach to the established canons of knowledge and culture, which tend to be seen as manifestations of a Western, patriarchal outlook, erected to the exclusion of other 'narratives' and ways of understanding the world. These two phenomena interact in fascinating ways, and it is in their commingling that the worst excesses of political correctness come into focus.

Not that PC is all bad — far from it. In many ways, political correctness is a natural and even healthy outgrowth of something not always noted in our society: the gap between the language of equality and the reality of inequality. Unfairness and discrimination survive the introduction of democracy, and in some ways become more conspicuous because of it. The French political thinker Alexis de Tocqueville was early on the point: '[M]en will never establish any equality with which they can be contented,' he wrote in *Democracy in America*. 'When inequality of conditions is the common law of society, the most marked inequalities do not strike the eye; when everything is nearly on the same level, the slightest are marked enough to hurt it.'[9] There can be no social justice without political freedom. But the first thing does not follow inevitably from the second, and political correctness is an (often clumsy) attempt to bridge the gap between the two.

In an essay on the poet Philip Larkin, the British novelist Martin Amis — an author who has often found himself indicted on grounds of political incorrectness by the kind of critic who has trouble understanding the difference between exploring human ugliness and celebrating or recommending it — provides some excellent thoughts on PC. Here, he addresses the charge of racism, though his words would apply to sexism, too, or to any other form of prejudice:

> Although it is French in its philosophical origins, PC begins with the very American — and attractive and honourable — idea that no one should feel ashamed of what he was born as, of what he is ... Viewed at its grandest, PC is an attempt to accelerate evolution. To speak truthfully, while that's still okay, everybody is 'racist', or has racial prejudices. This is because human beings tend to like the similar, the familiar, the familial. I am a racist; I am not as racist as my parents; my children will not be as racist as I am ... Freedom from racism is what we hope for, down the line. Impatient with this hope, this process, PC seeks to get the thing done right now — in a generation. To achieve this, it will need a busy executive wing, and much invigilation. What it will actually entrain is another ton of false consciousness, to add to the megatons of false consciousness already aboard, and then a backlash.[10]

What interests me is Amis' description of the impetus *behind* PC, the 'very American — and attractive and honourable — idea that no one should feel ashamed of what he was born as, of what he is'. Overlooking the very un-PC use of 'he' as a gender-neutral pronoun, that's as good a description of the spirit of political correctness as we're likely to come across, though it leaves unanswered — unasked — the question of why PC developed when it did.

Of Liberty and Liberation

'We hold these truths to be self-evident,' begins the US Declaration of Independence, 'that all men are created equal; that they are endowed by their Creator with certain unalienable Rights, that among these are Life, Liberty and the pursuit of Happiness.' A noble sentiment, nobly expressed. And yet the form of words adopted and ratified by the Continental Congress in 1776 was, in one particular at least, more than a little disingenuous.

For what the Founding Fathers failed to mention — though they'd discussed it at length among themselves — was that in throwing off the chains of Empire, they would leave untouched a pervasive system in which men were very far from equal, in which men (and women and children) were reduced to the status of property, of chattels. And not only would they leave it untouched; some of them would continue to profit from it. The man who had drafted the Declaration, Thomas Jefferson, owned hundreds of slaves — men at 'liberty' to do nothing more than work on his tobacco plantation in Virginia. To describe this as a double standard would be to put it delicately. There is a species of ditzy commentator that likes to talk as if this or that event — Pearl Harbor, Vietnam, Watergate, 9/11 — represents 'the loss of American innocence'. But there was never any innocence to lose. Slavery is America's original sin.

But what the Declaration did do was give the abolitionists a language with which to challenge slavery, a language less ambiguous than the religious one they had so far favoured. If all men were 'created equal', why, they asked, was it possible for a black man to be bought and sold as a commodity by a white one? Seeking to protect their economic investment, slaveholders fell back on the argument that African Americans were only partly human, which must have sounded disingenuous even in the 18th century. The English abolitionist Thomas Day put the matter in picturesque terms: 'If there be an object truly ridiculous in nature,' he wrote in 1776, 'it is an American patriot, signing resolutions of independency with the one hand, and with the other brandishing a whip over his affrighted slaves.'[11]

It was *because* the Declaration of Independence illuminated this blatant hypocrisy that it continued to serve as an inspiration to anti-racists throughout the 19th and 20th centuries. When Dr Martin Luther King led the civil-rights movement in the 1950s and 1960s, he laced his speeches and writings with references to the Founding Fathers and their literature. In his 'Letter from Birmingham Jail', for example, he portrayed the struggle for civil rights as the true inheritor of the framers' vision:

One day the South will know that when these disinherited children of God sat down at lunch counters, they were in reality standing up for what is best in the American dream and for the most sacred values in our Judaeo-Christian heritage, thereby bringing our nation back to those great wells of democracy which were dug deep by the founding fathers in their formulation of the Constitution and the Declaration of Independence.[12]

For Dr King, the answer to racial injustice was to stress the essential bond between human beings. As he put it in his 'I Have a Dream' speech, people should be judged not by the colour of their skin but by 'the content of their character'. But for others, frustrated by the slow pace of change, this was naïve idealism. Looking abroad, they saw another model emerging — one in which difference became the *focus* of resistance, rather than something to be overcome. Here, native peoples in Africa and elsewhere sought to expel their imperial oppressors not by denying their nativeness but by accentuating and embracing it. As the literary theorist Edward Said put it, 'If blacks had once been stigmatized and given inferior status to whites, then it has since become necessary not to deny blackness, and not to aspire to whiteness, but to accept and celebrate blackness.'[13] In short, what those frustrated African Americans saw was nationalism with a racial focus, and it was to just such a model that many of them now turned in an effort to restore community pride. Taking their leave of the civil-rights movement, of social democratic intellectuals, of the unions, and of the Democratic Party, African Americans began to embrace what would eventually be called identity politics.

Of course, African Americans weren't the only group to embrace identity politics in the 1960s and 1970s. Feminists began to see that formal rights and democracy would not be enough to overcome sexism; that to do this it would be necessary to challenge cultural assumptions, to confront 'social constructions' of femininity. Similarly, gay men and lesbians sought to counter homophobic prejudice by eschewing 'gay rights' and adopting instead the more radical goal of 'sexual liberation'. And while these movements differed in many ways, they shared a frustration with traditional liberalism; with incremental, rights-based activism. Democracy may be able to deliver on universal suffrage and property rights, but what it cannot do, these radicals insisted, is bring about genuine equality. In order to achieve that, and to engender pride, it was necessary to tackle the dominant ideology, which was all the more dominant for being invisible.

In the late 1960s and the 1970s, these movements were considered to be on the radical fringe of a left that still had as item one on its agenda the improvement of workers' pay and conditions. But as the 20th century approached its terminus, this situation began to change. As the right started to win the economic arguments, mainstream leftists looked around for other stars to hitch their wagons to. Sections of the traditional left began to refocus their ideological efforts away from issues of economics and class, and towards the politics of ethnicity and gender. As the British cultural theorist Stuart Hall has noted, 'shared social identity' and not material interest became the mobilising factor for many on the left.[14]

This is where political correctness comes in. A key way in which this New Left sought to confront cultural stereotypes and overcome racial or gender prejudice was by challenging the taken-for-granted assumptions of the society in which these prejudices persisted. For this, it would need not banners and placards but what Amis called 'invigilation'. And where better to invigilate than in a university?

Canon Fodder

Foxes live in dens and rabbits live in warrens. And leftwing radicals live in universities. A stereotype, but a plausible one. Political correctness is as bound up with academia as the film industry is with Hollywood, and, according to its sternest critics, just as reliant on fantasy.

When it comes to university education, political correctness tends to work on two levels. First, there is its effect on the institutions themselves, on the day-to-day running of universities. We've all heard of university speech codes, whereby staff and students are required to avoid certain offensive words and expressions upon pain of disciplinary action, or worse. The stated aim of these codes is to create an environment in which disadvantaged groups are free from conspicuous prejudice. But for many commentators their principal effect is not to resolve grievances but to keep them alive, to act as the focus for political agitation and engender an atmosphere of mutual surveillance. Paul Berman has written of the 'small-time inquisitions' favoured by many professors and students, while his fellow political commentator Todd Gitlin has identified 'a bitter intolerance' on much of the academic left.[15] This is one of the key problems with PC: in moving beyond political liberalism, it opens the door to *illiberal* attitudes. Censors, even when they say they are fighting against intolerance and bigotry, do not seek freedom from others' views but the freedom to impose their own, and the combination of democratic rhetoric and anti-democratic attitudes make the PC animal ripe for satire.[16]

In her excellent book *Heterophobia*, Daphne Patai looks at the growth of the idea of sexual harassment on US campuses, noting how male lecturers are targeted by zealous female students in thrall to an idea of society as reflexively phallo- and hetero-centric.[17] In her class on women's utopian fiction, many of her female students speak approvingly of the Christian fundamentalist version of the United States set out in Margaret Atwood's *The Handmaid's Tale*. It may be a totalitarian system — one in which a woman's 'sexuality' denotes only her reproductive potential and in which pleasure (physical and romantic) has been banished. But at least the women don't have to put up with wolf whistles and sexual innuendo! Thus the struggle against discrimination morphs all too easily into admiration for the most oppressive systems imaginable.[18]

Agitation at the institutional level is, for Patai, inseparable from the question of what is taught in universities, which brings us to the second level at which political correctness operates. PC has been called 'political etiquette', as if it were merely a species of decorum;[19] but this is to ignore its philosophical underpinnings. Clearly, the 'sexual harassment industry' (as Patai describes it) is closely related to a particular view of sexuality and gender relations as socially constructed, and it is only when we consider these underlying issues that we can really get to grips with political correctness.

In the 1980s and 1990s, it was to the study of literature that PC attitudes clung most tenaciously. There is no obvious reason for this, though I suspect that it has a lot to do with the increasingly vocational emphasis in education. I can only speak for the United Kingdom, but it is clear to me that by the early 1990s the idea of 'liberal' education was in abeyance, and that in the eyes of market-centric politicians leisure-class indulgences such as the appreciation of literature were about as useful as a chocolate fireguard. ('Oh, they still run those courses, do they?' my new housemate — an aeronautical engineer — said when I told him I was studying English literature.) There was therefore something defensive about the way in which literature departments turned themselves into theoretical enclaves: we were doing something important, and the way you could tell we were doing something important was that you didn't have a clue what we were on about. Suddenly, 'A Study of Thomas Hardy's Wessex' became 'The Phallocentric Pastoral: deconstructing Thomas Hardy's landscapes'. Needless to say, neither study would land us a cushy job in the city. But at least the second would allow us to believe that we were laying bare the oppressive nature of the system that deemed us irrelevant, and, in so doing, we were manuring the ground for a future transformation of society. So put *that* in your glass of Bollinger and sip it!

'[M]y subject,' wrote Catharine R. Stimpson, the 1990 president of the US Modern Language Association (widely regarded as the global headquarters of PC studies in the 1990s), 'is the study of the modern languages and literatures as a drama of difference.'[20] For Stimpson, the new emphasis in literary studies reflected the changing nature of society. Traditionally, of course, the Western academy had been in thrall to the so-called canon, the loosely defined collection of texts — beginning with the ancient Greeks and ending with the high modernists of the 20th century — the significance of which was apparently not in question among those whose taste accounted for anything. With a few exceptions (Sappho, George Eliot), the writers on this list were white and male, a fact that seemed to reflect and reinforce a Western-centred, patriarchal outlook. And so academics increasingly began to specialise in the 'literatures' outside this tradition: in indigenous literature, in female literature, in postcolonial literature. In this sense, academic political correctness amounted to a broadening and a democratisation, a focus that, in Stimpson's words, '[promised] to bring dignity to the dispossessed and self-empowerment to the disempowered, to recuperate the texts and traditions of ignored groups, to broaden cultural history'.[21]

This was not a fruitless project. A wealth of unimagined riches accrued to Western literature departments, increasing our knowledge and understanding of the world, and throwing our own experience into relief. And yet what some academics seemed to look forward to was not a widening of the literary canon but an assault on the principles underlying it. The problem with the canon was not that it was incomplete; the problem was that it was *the canon* — the literary record, so to speak, of white, male, European oppression. One studied it, when one studied it at all, only in order to 'demythologise' it, to tease out its racist, misogynistic undertones. Literary considerations, in short, took a back seat to ideological ones.

Again, I am flirting with a stereotype here. But there really was a species of student — and likely still is — for whom there was a direct line from Plato to NATO. The history of the West, such students reasoned, is the history of domestic and foreign oppression. And Western literature reflects that history. It is the job of the literary academic to say so, and to liberate the voices of the dispossessed into the mainstream.[22]

As the US critic Irving Howe suggested, this vision of literature was predicated on a confusion of two kinds of hierarchy:

A social hierarchy may entail a (mal)distribution of income and power, open to the usual criticisms; a literary 'hierarchy' signifies a judgment, often based on historical experience, that some works are of supreme or abiding value, while others are of lesser value, and still others quite without value.[23]

Of course, intelligent literary critics are not blind to the fact that works of literature reflect the ideological assumptions of the societies in which they have been written. But that is not all they do. They also deal with universal themes such as love and honour, hatred and revenge. And they do this in ways that are sometimes so original that they throw us into a new relationship with the world. When this happens, we say that the work has 'value'. Sometimes we call its author 'great'. And in doing this we necessarily set both the work and the author in a (mutable) hierarchy. In other words, we value literature *as literature* and not as ideological documentation. Evelyn Waugh was a great novelist. He was also an insufferable snob. And while his snobbery was not incidental to his art (and in *Brideshead Revisited* is not helpful to it), it certainly doesn't invalidate it. Literature is 'elitist', as are all the arts, but not in the same sense that societies are elitist.

Why so many on the academic left found this distinction hard to absorb is often difficult to understand. Until, that is, we remember that PC is a *political* phenomenon first. The most zealous PC academics didn't want a renaissance in the academy; they wanted a revolution outside of it.

If the canon had value, these academics assumed, then the culture from which it had sprung must have value too. Since none of them was willing to admit *that*, the whole notion of value had to go. And here they had an ace up their sleeves in the form of European critical theory, a set of philosophical ideas that would act (and still acts) as a powerful solvent on the traditional, hierarchical conception of literature.

Reality as Discourse

Political correctness is not merely the projection of identity politics into the academy, but the intermingling of identity politics and (largely) French critical theory. It is the confluence of two kinds of radicalism, one political and one philosophical. In short, it is where identity politics meets what's known as post-structuralism.

At the heart of post-structuralism is a conception of language that seems, on the face of it, perfectly reasonable. The idea is that meaning is unstable. In contrast to George Orwell's famous description of good prose as being like a pane of glass, words are not windows onto the world; they do not *suffer* reality but are permanently engaged in re-creating it. The word 'stone' is not an actual stone but a sort of promissory note; the stone that flashes up in my mind when I read or hear the word 'stone' will not be the same as the one in *your* mind when you read or hear it. So far so obvious. But post-structuralism takes this insight and expands it into a guiding principle. It says that since we inevitably bring our subjectivities to this or that text, 'the text' cannot be said to exist. What exists is an infinite number of readings in which the author's intention is necessarily secondary to the reader's interpretation. And, needless to say, that interpretation will be shaped by a number of social factors, including gender, race, and class.[24]

The effects of this theoretical outlook on English departments were revolutionary. Not only did it allow students of literature to disregard the notion of value, but it also allowed those students to focus on political and philosophical questions, rather than on literary ones. Instead of treating works of literature as discrete arrangements of content and form — intimately related to the societies from which they had sprung, but also in some ways separable from them, of interest in and of themselves — students saw them as opportunities to discuss the ways in which race and gender (and sometimes class) were instrumental in creating meaning. Criticism became an exercise in consciousness-raising. What mattered was not a work's literary merit, nor even a work's (intended) meaning, but what it told you about the *creation* of meaning and the relative nature of truth in general. And it is *this* approach to truth and language, incubated in English departments, that would soon bleed out into other disciplines, and ultimately beyond the university's walls.

No doubt many academics would regard this sketch as irredeemably crude. But irredeemably crude was *what you got* in the literary departments of the 1990s. Derrida is a far more subtle philosopher than many of his critics give him credit for, but those in thrall to his philosophical method tended to lack the intellectual equipage to turn those ideas to advantage in essays about *Hard Times* and *Mary Barton*. In his excellent book *The Trouble with Theory*, academic and author Gavin Kitching analyses a stack of undergraduate papers to tease out the assumptions underlying them. Though sympathetic to many of the views espoused by his academic charges, Kitching regards post-structuralism as a philosophical dead-end — at least as it is pursued by most undergraduates. For him, the typical undergraduate essay automatically assumes that the world is a subjective construct, but this theoretical position is rarely followed to its logical conclusion. ('If the world is a subjective construct — a creation of politicised discourse — in what sense is my view of it superior to anyone else's?') As Kitching puts it: 'They write theses of the form 'language constructs the social world in this way (singular) but I see through this construction and reject it'. But, of course, if they can see through the construction and reject it, why (one might ask) can others not do so too? And if others do do so, then in what sense is the construction socially or politically dominant?'[25]

Words clearly have power, argues Kitching. But power is not a property of words; it is a property of the people who manipulate them. And while an awareness of your own subjectivity is a useful thing to have before entering upon any intellectual journey, to treat objectivity as ideology is to concede defeat before you've pulled on your boots.

Students, writes Kitching, 'have been led down the path to philosophical incoherence by righteous indignation'. Post-structuralism is politically self-defeating.

But the point is not students' incoherence, nor their shaky grasp of French theory. The point is that they became enamoured of a view of reality as determined by 'discourse'. And it is this view, married to identity politics, that really set the PC cat among the plump academic pigeons.

Nor could the cat be crammed back into its bag. Though it felt most at home in the literature departments, this peculiar mindset soon ventured outside them, rubbing around the legs of the other humanities and eventually even curling up with the hard sciences. The central idea was that *all* human knowledge must be the result of discourse; that even physics and biology are projections of patriarchal, Western culture; that there are no non-theoretical facts that are simply *there* awaiting discovery; that truth, to put it simply, is relative. In his 1998 essay 'Oppressed by Evolution', American anthropologist Matt Cartmill gives an excellent summary of this worldview:

> The postmodern critique of science runs something like this: There are no objective facts. All supposed 'facts' are contaminated with theories, and all theories are infested with moral and political doctrines. Because different theories express different perceptions of the world, there's no neutral yardstick for measuring one against another. The choice between competing theories is always a political choice.

Therefore, when some guy in a lab coat tells you that such and such is an objective fact — say, that there isn't any firmament, or that people are related to wolves and hyenas — he must have a political agenda up his starched white sleeve.[26]

This outlook was most famously satirised by the physics professor Alan Sokal, who in 1996 claimed to have seen the postmodern light and conned the US journal *Social Text* into printing an essay entitled 'Transgressing the Boundaries: towards a transformative hermeneutics of quantum gravity'. The essay proposed that physical reality was a social and linguistic construct, and that the discoveries of quantum physics had progressive political implications. Among other points just as ludicrous, Sokal argued that it was necessary to reject the 'elite caste's' imposition of its 'canon of "high science"' and embrace an 'emancipatory mathematics'.[27]

In short, what the PC hardliners did was to treat all information as political. Knowledge, they argued, was not monolithic but subject to the vagaries of culture. In fact, there was no such thing as knowledge; there were only individual 'knowledges'. And these knowledges, far from being complementary, were in fact in competition with each other. 'He who receives an idea from me,' wrote Thomas Jefferson in 1813, 'receives instruction himself without lessening mine; as he who lights his taper at mine, receives light without darkening mine.'[28] 'Bullshit!' said the PC academics, before pointing out that as an owner of slaves, Jefferson was hardly a credible source.

This outlook, often called relativism, is very closely bound up with reactionary attitudes, and nowhere is this more apparent than in the effect of PC upon the study of history. In the historical sphere the idea of knowledge as inescapably political — and thus as infinitely malleable — reached its ridiculous apogee.

Taking the Wish for the Reality

'Who controls the past controls the future,' wrote George Orwell in *Nineteen Eighty-Four*. This sinister formulation is one of the slogans belonging to the party of power, Ingsoc, and few real-world authoritarian governments would not recognise it as a statement of the obvious. Russian President Vladimir Putin takes a personal interest in the publication of 'patriotic' history textbooks, while in China the education department keeps a tight grip on the history taught in schools, which must stress the role of the Communist Party in delivering the Chinese people from slavery.[29] History, they know, is a high-stakes game. A little manipulation of it goes a long way.

It is for this reason that the teaching of history in the 1980s and 1990s became such a focus of leftwing academics in thrall to the principles of identity politics. As we've seen, the aim of political correctness is to liberate the disempowered from the overseers of the dominant culture. What higher prize could one envisage, then, than a version of the past that challenged the assumptions underlying traditional history and that restored some pride to those communities who had been ignored or marginalised by it?

In his absorbing book *It's a PC World*, the British author and broadcaster Edward Stourton makes the persuasive point that such a project is in one sense no different from the situation in the recent past: 'The case for a PC approach to history is very largely driven by the desire to create for everyone the kind of relationship with the past that I took for granted.'[30] Stourton, who was born in 1957, would have been taught a version of history in which the British Empire was more hero than villain, a version that most historians would now recognise as hopelessly naïve. But while many in the West were questioning its history — were finding out that the Industrial Revolution may have had as much to do with the movement of South American gold as it did with British ingenuity, or that victory in World War II owed more to the Russians than to the RAF — others were rewriting history to take account of forgotten peoples. At its best, this produced some necessary books: books that employed genuine scholarship in order to challenge orthodox history. But at its worst, it produced books that were grounded not in scholarship but in ideology and wishful thinking. And in this latter case, the idea that truth is relative came in very handy indeed.

The most well known (and most extreme) examples of this kind of history come under the heading 'Afrocentrism', an unimprovable description of which appears in Robert Hughes's *Culture of Complaint*, a splenetic account of modern American manners that anyone interested in political correctness should read:

> [Afrocentrism] says that the history of the cultural relations between Africa and Europe is bunk — a prop for the fiction of white European supremacy. Palaeohistorians generally agree that intelligent human life began in the Rift Valley of Africa. The Afrocentrist goes further: the African was the *cultural* father of us all. European culture derives from Egypt, and Egypt is part of Africa, linked to its heart by the artery of the Nile. Egyptian civilisation begins in sub-Saharan Africa, in Ethiopia and the Sudan.[31]

Thus, according to Cheikh Anta Diop, one of the pioneers of Afrocentrist history, it was Africans who invented the pyramid form, as well as hieroglyphics and the pillared temple. Similarly, Indus Khamit Kush has argued that the first mathematicians, scientists, astronomers, and physicians were black Africans, as indeed were Jesus and Muhammad.[32] To say that the evidence for these claims is scanty would be to put it mildly. But evidence can be unreliable and (as the African knows to his cost) is very often fabricated. And so we find proselytisers for Afrocentrism claiming that racist archaeologists mutilated the faces of Egyptian statues in order to disguise their Negroid features, and that the Greeks 'stole' philosophy, art, and religion (and no doubt the recipe for taramasalata) from the ancient Egyptians and passed them off as their own.[33] Thus do the blooms of racial self-confidence spring up from a mulch of conspiracy theories.

As Hughes suggests, such a historical outlook is essentially just a non-white version of the notion of manifest destiny, according to which 19th-century white Americans gave themselves permission to annex Native American land. It is history, in other words, in the service of ideology. Or, as Arthur Schlesinger Jr put it in *The Disuniting of America*, it is 'history as therapy' — history designed to bolster self-esteem.[34] Faced with a gap in academic performance between whites and blacks, or between blacks and Asians, the Afrocentrist seeks to compensate his racial constituency with the thought that mathematics, say, was pinched from the Nubians by unscrupulous Arabs. The psychology isn't complicated. Academic 'underachievement' and low socio-economic status — the legacies of racism, not of racial difference — become the occasion for fantasies of superiority. The same impulse that led members of the Nation of Islam to claim that blacks are genetically superior to whites led also to a version of history in which black Africans became the founding fathers not just of a nation but of civilisation itself.

Afrocentrism is a footnote in the history of history. But the assumptions underlying it have bled out into the wider culture. In the US in particular, the idea that history (and knowledge in general) should improve self-esteem is ubiquitous. Again, the record is not all bad; no one of any intelligence longs for the days of imperial hubris, of 'ignorant savages' and 'the white man's burden'. But in overturning reactionary attitudes, political correctness sets up in their stead a picture of the world that is also distorted, albeit in a different way. No less than cane-wielding Catholic nuns, PCers take a 'transformative' view of education, seeking to influence what children are taught with a view to challenging dominant ideology and shaping the future according to their agenda. The problem is that proportion and accuracy don't always lend themselves to this high-minded project. In which case, the course is clear: proportion and accuracy have to go.

Perhaps the best book on this subject is Diane Ravitch's *The Language Police*, which looks at the way in which various pressure groups attempt to influence the content of school textbooks and the policies of state education agencies in the United States. A historian of education and a member of the US National Assessment Governing Board between 1997 and 2004, Ravitch is well placed to comment on the phenomenon, which she defines as an 'elaborate, well-established protocol of beneficent censorship, quietly endorsed and broadly implemented by textbook publishers, testing agencies, professional associations, states, and the federal government'. Educational materials, she writes, 'are now governed by an intricate set of rules to screen out language and topics that might be considered controversial or offensive'.[35] While by no means restricted to criticisms of the left, *The Language Police* is most illuminating in its analyses of political correctness, of the well-meaning but misguided academics who attempt to cleanse educational material of all prejudicial overtones, even at the risk of presenting children with books and assignments with no grounding in reality. For example, Ravitch writes of the way in which 'bias and sensitivity review panels' are able to spike reading passages designed for use in examinations on the basis of the most 'absurd reasoning'. Thus a passage on the class distinctions that obtained in ancient Egypt — a passage that 'to the naked eye … was descriptive, not judgmental' — is rejected for its 'elitist' tone, while a passage about patchwork quilting by women on the western frontier in the mid 19th century is rejected because it represents women engaged in stereotypically female behaviour.[36] More generally, Ravitch notes the way in which the teaching of history has come to reflect a broadly PC agenda. For example, World War II is frequently taught as an episode in the struggle for women's rights as opposed to an episode in the struggle against fascism, while the counterculture of the 1960s is depicted as an unambiguously good thing, as opposed to a phenomenon about which there are strong disagreements and which many consider to be responsible for the rise of social ills, such as the drug culture and marital breakdown.

In most modern textbooks, Ravitch contends, no one is at a disadvantage. In this sense, description is confused with judgement, as bureaucrats and publishers conspire to create an entirely inoffensive world, one in which there is a 'balanced representation' of people from different racial groups, in which men and women have the same abilities, and in which anything that is controversial or upsetting is removed in order to protect self-esteem. In short, the wish is taken for the reality: kids from ethnic minorities are shown positive versions of their own communities, and female students encouraged to transcend their history of subjugation not through an honest analysis of that history but through a partial account of it. Hughes calls this 'remedial belief': rather than dealing with the world as it is, teachers present students with the world as it might be, as if one could right the wrongs of history simply by rewriting it.[37]

The absurdity of this approach is that it leads us away from the very knowledge needed to truly understand racism, or sexism, or economic disadvantage. As Ravitch puts it, 'The sanitising of world history texts has stripped them of their ability to present a critical, intellectually honest assessment of controversial subjects. On almost any subject relating to today's world, the texts strive so hard to be positive that they are misleading and inaccurate.'[38] Born of the desire to overcome prejudice, PC creates a situation in which prejudice cannot be openly discussed, let alone intelligently analysed. Indeed, the legacy of knowledge as therapy is a state of mind no therapist should tolerate: a state of mind in which denial and repression block the entrance to genuine self-knowledge.

The idea that history can be used to bolster the self-esteem of the weak is also apt to provoke a backlash from the strong, with the result that the truth recedes even further.

Affronted (or offended) by the attempt to turn history into a tool of social engineering, conservatives push back with their own agenda. In the United Kingdom, the sense that the teaching of history is infected with PC attitudes has led to a huge resurgence of interest in Edwardian books such as *Our Island Story*, which takes it for granted that the British Empire is (or rather was) on the side of the angels.[39] Similarly, in Australia, political correctness in Aboriginal historiography is exaggerated by conservative historians bent on reaffirming (and reinstating) their own vision. Indeed, the backlash against PC history reminds us that the desire to *tailor* the past to the needs of a particular group is an essentially reactionary one. Again, and as both Stourton and Hughes argue, political correctness will sometimes mirror the very system it seeks to reform.

The Cheating Language of Equality

Of course, one way in which political correctness does differ from the conservative outlook is in the radical approach it takes to language. Growing out of an idea of reality as ultimately determined by (political) discourse, PC regards language as both the incubator of prejudice and the means to its eradication. But again, the attempt to engender verbal hygiene is apt not only to distort reality but also to make reality impossible to discuss.

Take one example. In 1884, Mark Twain published a novel that established him as a writer of genius and put his country on the literary map. It was called *Adventures of Huckleberry Finn* and it tells the story of a resourceful teenager who runs away from his abusive father and hooks up with another runaway, Jim — a black man attempting to make his way from the slave state of Missouri to the free state of Ohio in order to buy his family's freedom. Its theme is racism, and its power resides in the portrayal of its protagonist, a boy brought up to accept slave ownership but morally clearheaded enough to treat his companion with dignity and friendship, and to help him in his quest for liberty. In the words of its author, the message of the book is that in matters of morality 'a sound heart is a safer guide than an ill-trained conscience'.[40]

The book was both a popular and a critical success, but not everyone was enamoured of it. Objections were raised in the name of public morality: the novel's language was coarse and inelegant; its teenage narrator was a lowlife; its plot was awash with petty thefts and lies, not to mention denigrations of religion and respectability. But from behind the perfumed handkerchief pressed ostentatiously to the nose and lips, something else was evident — a snarl of resentment that the racist attitudes which survived the Emancipation Proclamation had been challenged. Amid all the talk of shonky grammar, dodgy morals, and indecent conduct, one could still discern the authentic plaint of antebellum Southern America.

Jump forward about a hundred years, to the 1980s and 1990s, when a different objection to the novel was raised — not for the first time, but with a force and frequency previously unseen. On this occasion, it wasn't a reactionary objection but a supposedly progressive one. According to many academics and commentators, the book was guilty of the thing its author sought to condemn: racism. And while some of these academics and commentators tried to start a useful discussion about whether Twain had fully transcended the attitudes he purported to hate, others were not so subtle in their reasoning. For them the 'racism' of the book was reducible to a single word beginning with 'n', worming through the text like a maggot in an apple, and just as indigestible to those whose ideological stomachs are, so to speak, on the sensitive side.

So, let's recapitulate. In the late 19th century, Mark Twain wrote a book that changed the way many Americans thought about race. And in the late 20th century the book was proscribed — removed, in many cases, from American syllabi — on the grounds that it contained a racist epithet. I think that deserves the name of irony. Or as Huck himself might prefer to say, 'Well, there ain't no sense in it.'

Nor has the controversy gone away. As recently as 2011, Professor Alan Gribben produced an edition of Twain's novel from which the word 'nigger' had been removed, suggesting that since its prevalence was preventing teachers from teaching the novel, and sensitive readers from reading it, the best thing to do was to get rid of it altogether. (In his version, the word is replaced with 'slave'.) No doubt Gribben's intentions were benign, but the fact is his actions were not only ruinous to the texture of Twain's vernacular;

they were also corrosive of his moral purpose. The subjects of Twain's novel are racism and slavery. As such, the book affords an opportunity to discuss the circumstances in which the word 'nigger' came to be so reviled. To remove the word makes no sense at all. It is an invitation to amnesia.

This is not to deny the pain the word can cause. Like a lump of linguistic polonium, 'nigger' radiates injustice and obloquy as no other word in the English language. But its proscription in such educational contexts (as opposed to purely social ones) is revealing of a deep confusion. There is no doubt that language reinforces prejudice. When a woman is required to adopt a title that broadcasts her marital status to the world, a message is sent that that woman's identity is in some sense determined by her relationship with men. In that sense, language alters reality, or affects our interpretation of it.[41] But in thrall as it is to a notion of language as inseparable from reality, political correctness, as I've defined it, goes further. It says that there is no real difference between, say, writing or saying the word 'nigger' and treating black people as inferior to white people. For a black person hearing or reading the word, the language and the reality are identical.

This confusion is perfectly caught, for me, in Howard Jacobson's novel *The Finkler Question*, which won the 2010 Man Booker Prize. The novel's protagonist is Julian Treslove, a man with what can only be described as a complicated attitude to Jews and Jewishness. But Treslove doesn't call Jews 'Jews'; he calls them 'Finklers', after his (Jewish) friend Finkler. Why? Because, according to Treslove, the word 'Jew' is 'small and dark and beetling' — just as he imagined Jews to be before he'd ever (knowingly) met one. It doesn't occur to him that his ideas about Jews may have coloured his view of the word 'Jew', or that his disordered relationship with Jewishness would survive the introduction of an alternative word. (Spoiler alert: it does.) In short, he fails sufficiently to grasp the fact that the reality of racial prejudice *precludes* the language through which it is expressed.[42]

The PCer seeks, in T. S. Eliot's phrase, 'to purify the dialect of the tribe'. In this he is not only doomed to failure; he is also fated to distort reality. The late historian and essayist Tony Judt, afflicted in his final years by the paralysing Lou Gehrig's disease, put this as well as anyone. In an interview with the *London Review of Books*, he denounced the appellation 'differently abled' to describe disabled people such as himself. His objection to the label was a political one: those who employ it are attempting to deny or to downplay the serious inequalities between people with different capacities: 'You describe everyone as having the same chances when actually some people have more chances than others. And with this cheating language of equality deep inequality is allowed to happen much more easily.'[43]

Faith in the Future

Putting the case against political correctness, Robert Hughes writes: 'We want to create a sort of linguistic Lourdes, where evil and misfortune are dispelled by a dip in the waters of euphemism.'[44] Obviously that superb analogy has particular resonance in Judt's case; but what I like is the suggestion of superstition, the idea that PC is born of faith and not of reason. The faith is not in God, of course, but in a certain idea of the future — a future in which everyone has the same 'life chances' and no one is at a disadvantage, economically or otherwise, to anyone else. And so compelling is this vision of the future that everything in the intellectual sphere must be geared to making it a reality. Literature, history, science, language — all are required to do their bit, to shoulder their burden, on the road to the Just City.

That road is paved with good intentions. Political correctness grows out of a desire to right past wrongs, wrongs that continue into the present, and it is for this reason that so many on the left, though they would never have welcomed the designation 'PC', were seduced by its underlying strictures. But what PC has done is to create a situation in which certain problems, far from being resolved, cannot even be sensibly discussed, and in which a focus on language — on how we *talk* about issues — comes to obscure, or even stand in for, real and effective political action. That is what happens when the principles of the Enlightenment take a backseat to our sense of entitlement. We do not advance the cause of justice. We just make *injustice* harder to see.

CHAPTER THREE

Fighting Ire with Ire

*The right has its own form of PC ... equally designed to veil
unwelcome truths. It, too, has a vested interest in keeping America
divided, a strategy that bodes worse for the country's polity than
anything the weak, constricted American left can be blamed for.*

ROBERT HUGHES, *CULTURE OF COMPLAINT*

It was on a winter's day back in 1986 that the icy winds
of political correctness announced themselves to the Great
British Public, chilling it to the commonsensical bone and
freezing its features into a rictus of disgust. The following
story appeared under the byline of Bill Akass of the *Daily
Star*:

Toddlers have been ordered to stop singing Baa Baa Black
Sheep ... because it is racist. Staff at a nursery school in
Hackney, London, claim the traditional nursery rhyme is
offensive to blacks. At first they wanted the 30 children aged
between one and three — only two of whom are black —
to sing Baa Baa White Sheep instead. But now it has been
banned altogether at Beevers Nursery in De Beauvoir Road.

Leaders of Left-wing Hackney council welcomed the ban last night. A spokesman said: 'We consider playgroups and nurseries should be discouraged from singing the rhyme. It reinforces a derogatory and subservient use of the word "black" among our youngsters in their formative years. This is particularly important because the majority of children in our nurseries come from black and ethnic minority communities.'[1]

Needless to say, this extraordinary scoop proved to have more legs than a centipede, appearing in a rival tabloid under the headline 'Lefties Baa Black Sheep', and in many other publications besides. (Even *Knitting International*, a magazine not known for satire but with strong opinions on coloured wool, chipped in with some comments on 'equal tonality'.) Inspired by the suggestion that Beevers Nursery had originally intended to change the rhyme to 'Baa Baa White Sheep', some of the more creative journalists went into print with PC versions of this and other nursery rhymes. Perhaps, opined Ireland's *Sunday World*, 'Old MacDonald Had a Farm' should be rechristened 'Senior Citizen MacDonald Had a Rural Collective', and 'Old Mother Hubbard Went to the Cupboard' retitled 'Old Socially Disadvantaged Single Mother Hubbard Went to the Cupboard'. And then, of course, came the letter-writers, banging the sword of Plain Speaking against the shield of Common Sense: 'Will we be expected to feel odd when buying a ticket to — *dare I say it* — Blackfriars, or even Whitechapel?'[2] (Cue an over-the-top comparison with Mao's Red Guards or the Moscow Trials.)

The Hackney story was shocking enough. But when similar reports began to emerge from elsewhere in the nation's capital, the press went into a feeding frenzy. In October, for example, the *Daily Mail* — an unambiguously conservative sheet obsessed with British royalty — reported that the council in the borough of Haringey had banned 'Baa Baa Black Sheep' and mandated 'Baa Baa Green Sheep' instead.[3] Similarly, in February 1987 it was reported in the *Islington Gazette* that staff at a local nursery had objected to a boy singing the original rhyme and that his mother had pulled him out of the school as a result. The boy, Daniel Griffin, was handicapped, ensuring that the story was picked up nationally, with several dailies trying to outdo each other in point of outrage and lachrymosity. 'Baa Baa Nursery Ban on Sad Little Dan' wept the headline in Rupert Murdoch's *Sun*, which was determined to spare its readers nothing. 'Handicapped tot Daniel Griffin delighted his mum by reciting Baa Baa Black Sheep but loony leftie teachers banned it — for being racist!' The following day, the newspaper described the treatment of 'little Daniel' as 'sick' and conferred upon the offending council the title of Britain's 'vilest'.[4]

There was just one problem with this cluster of stories: most of them were bogus. Save for one or two details, none of the abovementioned stories checks out. Beevers did *not* ban 'Baa Baa Black Sheep' or contemplate replacing it with a politically correct rendering; it merely used alternative versions in order to keep the kids interested and amused. The council spokesman to whom Akass talked was unaware of this activity and, not wanting to embarrass the school, had sought to defend the supposed ban. That he did so in such preposterous terms lent credence to a story that should never have been written, but in later reports the spokesman's *response* is taken for the council's *policy* when in fact it was nothing of the kind. (Even if it were, this would not affect Beevers, which was run by parents and not by the council.)[5] Nor does the 'Green Sheep' story stand up. The *Mail* could adduce no evidence for its claim that the council had banned 'Baa Baa Black Sheep', let alone replaced it with a different rhyme.[6] The only story with a skerrick of truth in it was the one concerning the school in Islington, where teachers did indeed ditch the rhyme, though only because they believed that it was council policy to do so — a belief surely fuelled by the plethora of reports suggesting that such a ban was in place.[7] In short, this constellation of scandals — which originated in a low-rent tabloid in thrall to football and celebrity gossip, and better known for its exposés of the female form than its investigative journalism — was based on rumour, false allegation, and wilful misapprehension of the facts.

Not every newspaper was sold on these reports. The black paper *The Voice* saw through them immediately, detecting in the media pile-on a barefaced attempt to discredit leftwing councils and their policies on raising racial awareness. Certainly the press was on the hunt for stories about what it described as the 'loony left', whose obsession with minority and fringe issues and (often imaginary) racial and sexual 'problems' was a key focus in the general election of June 1987, in which the Thatcher-led Conservative Party was returned to power. Nor were all these stories baseless. Peter Jenkins, a respected columnist for the left-of-centre *Guardian* newspaper, wrote a number of pieces on the more ridiculous policies of certain leftwing councils in London, such as the ban imposed by Haringey council on anything but Nicaraguan coffee, and Lambeth council's removal of the word 'family' from its literature because it was 'discriminatory'.[8] But the fact remains that the nursery-rhyme story was almost wholly fabricated. It was 'political correctness gone mad' gone mad.

And yet the Black Sheep yarn has proven remarkably tenacious. More than a decade after the Islington debacle, conservative newspapers were still referring to it in an effort to discredit the Labour MP and former council leader Margaret Hodge.[9] Furthermore, in 2006 a new version of the 'controversy' appeared in the press: two pre-school nurseries in Oxfordshire were reported as having changed the rhyme to 'Baa Baa Rainbow Sheep'. Again, they were accused of political correctness; again, it emerged that the rhyme had been changed not for reasons of racial sensitivity but in order to improve the children's vocabulary.[10] The story has even popped up in Australia. Under the headline '"Racist" Baa Baa Black Sheep Put Out to Pasture', the

Queensland *Sunday Mail* reported in 2011 that some schoolchildren in north Queensland now sang different versions of the rhyme, though, again, the paper produced not a shred of evidence to suggest that this was the result of political correctness. On the contrary, the article contained a number of quotes from teachers suggesting the opposite: that the traditional rhyme had *not* been banned and that the activity of changing certain words had been conceived of as a fun way to enhance children's language skills. Indeed, notwithstanding a few asides about parallel 'controversies' in the United Kingdom, there is nothing in the article that justifies the headline.[11]

On the rare occasions I've mentioned to a stranger that I'm writing a book on offence and respect, my interlocutor has almost invariably referred to the 'Baa Baa Black Sheep' legend, or else to some other tempest in a teapot that turns out upon closer inspection to be either greatly exaggerated or completely false. Didn't they rename black bin liners once? Weren't manhole covers rechristened 'personhole covers'? Wasn't the word 'blackboard' declared beyond the pale? Well, no, actually, and no, and no; all of those stories are complete fabrications — bullshit from beginning to end.

But the really interesting thing about these myths is not so much their falsity as the fact that they allow their promulgators to experience the very offendedness that they are ostensibly criticising. No less than political correctness itself, the campaign *against* political correctness is a form of offence-taking and offence-mongering — one with the power to stop debates dead and obscure important questions of prejudice. Borrowing from the playbook of political correctness, the anti-PCers adopt a victim mentality: the proselytisers for PC are not just wrongheaded; they are bullies intent on vandalising our values. That is why children are so often the focus of template controversies such as the nursery-rhyme story: their involvement guarantees maximum indignation. From this perspective, political correctness is not just loony; it is creepy and sinister. It attempts to inculcate habits of mind conducive to a view of the world that we, the right-thinking majority, do not share. Thus teachers are attacked for their lefty leanings, and *Sesame Street* for its liberal bias.[12] Such attacks may be self-satirising, but they play on genuine anxieties.

A self-pitying populism informs this vision. It is essential that political correctness be cast as the enemy of ordinary folk. Hence the anti-elitist language adopted by its staunchest critics, for whom words such as 'egghead', 'progressive', 'elite', and even 'intellectual' are terms of abuse. Frequently, the anti-PC writer will adopt the persona of embattled truth-teller holding back the armies of fashionable thinking. 'I'm not supposed to say this *but ...*' this guardian of common sense declares, before charging headlong into the fray. Never more exquisitely in his element than when laying into the smug leftists whose ideas have so corrupted the polity, or when evoking the methods of the Thought Police in ensuring ideological compliance, his tone is at once populist and self-regarding.

The campaigner against political correctness is both a man of the people and a solitary warrior.

The infuriating thing, from a leftist perspective, is that many of his points are valid. Some on the left are wont to claim that PC is a rightwing invention, a cudgel with which to whack progressives whenever they try to tackle issues of prejudice or inequality. Though not completely wrong, they're not completely right either. As we saw in the previous chapter, the ideological inanity that gripped the left in the 1980s and 1990s was real enough, and is still a force to be reckoned with. Yes, the Black Sheep story was a furphy. But it was a furphy that caught the public's imagination because it exemplified a *genuine* phenomenon. The question is: why did the right seek to exaggerate that phenomenon? Why was it necessary to take something ludicrous and make it appear more ludicrous still?

Dialectical Elegance

In order to put this overreaction to political correctness into context, it is necessary to go back a bit and consider the right's own history of offence-taking. Or perhaps 'the conservative element in society' is a better designation than 'the right', since it isn't necessarily rightwing to be offended by obscenity or blasphemy. Nevertheless, up until the 1960s you wouldn't hear many people complaining about racial or sexual stereotypes. Offence, when it was taken, tended to be taken about things such as profanity and sexual swearwords, or the undermining of 'family values'.

Even in the 20th century, the conservative push for control over young minds was quite as impressive, and quite as blatant, as anything done in the name of progressivism. As Diane Ravitch shows in *The Language Police*, producers of school textbooks are as apt to cop flak from advocates for the traditional family, religious values, and national pride as they are from advocates for greater sensitivity in matters of race or sexuality.[13] While progressives often idealise the future, conservatives often idealise the past, and are no less tenacious in standing up for their vision.

To anyone over 40, the idea that taking offence is the peculiar preserve of progressive councillors and lefty academics will — or should — sound preposterous. When I was growing up in England, by far the most conspicuous instances of offence-taking centred on the subject of religion. In 1977, for example, the dust was blown off a blasphemy law that most Britons didn't even know existed in order to prosecute the publisher of *Gay News*, which had printed a poem by James Kirkup entitled 'The Love That Dares to Speak Its Name' — a tedious bit of doggerel that describes a Roman centurion ravishing the corpse of Jesus Christ. A couple of years later, Monty Python's *Life of Brian* touched off a wave of religious protest in both the United Kingdom and the United States. The fact that the film was not only a send-up of religion but also of leftwing politics appeared to escape its detractors, who were happy to paint it as a gratuitous attack on religion and decency by countercultural trendies. (The Pythons' penchant for dressing up as women, John Cleese has since suggested, only made matters worse.)[14]

The point is that 'traditional values' did not go missing in the late 20th century. Yet as the centre of political gravity shifted, conservatives began to change their tactics. Political correctness was a challenge to their assumptions, but it also afforded an opportunity to press their claims in a different way. By promoting the notion of PC from a marginal phenomenon — a phenomenon primarily of the *academic* left — to a central and organised assault on society, they could push their own political vision while seeming to criticise an inane ideology. In other words, the conservative reaction to political correctness is not merely protective of 'mainstream values' and 'common sense'; it is knowingly ideological — a counteroffensive against the cultural left. Political correctness needed correcting. But what the right provided was an *overcorrection*.

'With dialectical elegance, a new radicalism aroused a new conservatism,' writes Todd Gitlin in his magisterial study of the US culture wars, *The Twilight of Common Dreams*.[15] Self-righteously appealing to the reasonable person's loathing for self-righteousness, conservatives were able to cast themselves as the critics of a new species of offence-taking, while arousing in their followers powerful feelings of offendedness. Against the relativism of the PC left, conservatives offered established verities, and a vision of the West as essentially beneficent. As Robert Hughes notes in *Culture of Complaint*, this latter emphasis is apt to mutate into an obnoxious species of nationalism. Running in tandem with political correctness, and ultimately traceable to the same Puritan heritage, was what Hughes calls 'patriotic correctness', the browbeating of political opponents for undermining national pride.[16] And since national pride is the very thing that cultural relativism calls into question, the dragon slayers of the conservative press were never more complacently dyspeptic than when taking some pinko academic to task for failing to call a spade a spade. In one sense, both sides needed each other. Political correctness and patriotic correctness were locked in an antagonistic tango.

Visigoths in Tweed

Though in many ways determinedly lowbrow, the conservative backlash did have its philosophers. One year after the Hackney nursery *didn't* ban 'Baa Baa Black Sheep', and as the British left continued to cop a shellacking from the rightwing press, an obscure American academic, a professor of philosophy and political science at the University of Chicago, went into print with a chunky tome entitled *The Closing of the American Mind*. Densely argued and grandiloquently written, this treatise was not the kind of thing that tended to do well with a non-specialist readership — a reality reflected in the fact that its publishers, Simon & Schuster, printed just 10,000 copies in February 1987. And yet by late spring the book was selling 25,000 copies a week. In the summer it reached the top of the US bestseller list, where it stayed for two-and-a-half months.

Described by Camille Paglia as 'the first shot in the culture wars',[17] the book was written by Professor Allan Bloom and lavishly subtitled 'how higher education has failed democracy and impoverished the souls of today's students'. Its thesis was that the American university had perverted, or was in the process of perverting, the traditional role of philosophy and the humanities, which it no longer regarded as repositories of truth but as opportunities to show how truth is bound by language and culture. In so doing, it had effectively turned its back on the ideal of a liberal-arts education, by which is meant those subjects and skills considered essential for a free-thinking person. Above all, the book was an attack on relativism. The American mind, the professor suggested, was closed precisely because it had become so *open*. As he put it:

> Openness used to be the virtue that permitted us to seek the good by using reason. It now means accepting everything and denying reason's power. The unrestrained and thoughtless pursuit of openness, without recognizing the inherent political, social, or cultural problem of openness as the goal of nature, has rendered openness meaningless.[18]

Notwithstanding the histrionic nature of many of Bloom's assertions, it is clear that *The Closing of the American Mind* identified a real phenomenon, and indeed a real problem: cultural relativism *had* given rise to new forms of dogmatism in the Western university. But Bloom was not only concerned with academia; he was also concerned to relate developments in academia to society at large. His book is laced with dyspeptic accounts of contemporary popular youth culture, some of which are so over the top that we begin to fear for the author's sanity. 'Whether it be Nuremberg or Woodstock,' he writes, 'the principle is the same. As Hegel was said to have died in Germany in 1933, Enlightenment in America came close to breathing its last during the sixties.' Or here he is on that 'demon' and 'teen-age satyr' Michael Philip Jagger:

> In his act he was male and female, heterosexual and homosexual; unencumbered by modesty, he could enter everyone's dreams, promising to do everything with everyone; and, above all, he legitimated drugs, which were the real thrill that parents and policemen conspired to deny his youthful audience. He was beyond the law, moral and political, and thumbed his nose at it.[19]

An exotic performance — and not just from Mick! But for Bloom there really was a connection between the 'gutter phenomenon' of pop music and the malaise within the American academy. Both revealed a situation in which genuine authority had ceased to be meaningful.

In many ways, Bloom's unlikely bestseller is not typical of the anti-PC genre. For one thing, it is a work of philosophy, grounded in an understanding of the Western philosophical canon (in contrast to the books inspired by it, which are rarely more philosophical than *The Very Hungry Caterpillar*). Moreover, Professor Bloom himself was certainly no poster boy for traditional values. A homosexual who died of AIDS, he lived a free-spending, sensuous lifestyle — hardly the kind of inclinations to endear him to conservative readers, the curtain-twitchers and capital-letter moralists who believe that what America needs is more families like the Waltons and fewer families like the Simpsons.[20] But *The Closing of the American Mind* was, as critic Michael Berubé put it in 1991, 'the jab that allowed the Right to set up the haymaker it's delivering now'.[21] Its focus on relativism, and on the way in which relativism was corrupting young minds, was just what post–Cold War conservatives needed.

For the anti-PCers, the self-styled counter-intelligentsia, the bottom-up revolution of the 1960s had become the top-down revolution of the 1980s and 1990s — a new totalitarianism. In the early 1990s, magazine articles delineated the PC phenomenon in what can only be described as hysterical terms. ('Are you politically correct?' asked *New York Magazine*, next to a photograph of book-burning Nazis. 'Watch What You Say. Thought Police' declared *Newsweek* on its front cover.) At the same time, a number of conservative authors went into print with books purporting to dish the dirt on the multiculturalists, feminists, homosexuals, Marxists, post-structuralists, and new historicists infesting the modern academy. Roger Kimball's *Tenured Radicals: how politics has corrupted our higher education* and Dinesh D'Souza's *Illiberal Education: the politics of race and sex on campus*, published in 1990 and 1991 respectively, were exemplary in this regard, and continue to have enormous influence. The counteroffensive against political correctness was, by this stage, quite as impressive as the phenomenon of political correctness itself.

Ostensibly, these books are descriptive, and defensive. The Western university, the argument goes, is under attack from the heirs of the counterculture, and the values of liberal education are in the process of being vandalised by what D'Souza calls the 'visigoths in tweed'. For Kimball, the multiculturalist ethos implies that all cultures are equally valuable — that the very idea of 'high culture' is naïve, elitist, and domineering. Consequently, to profess a preference for high culture and the Western canon is not only to invite accusations of racism (or sexism, or homophobia, or whatever) but also to run the risk of ostracism. In short, the ideal of 'disinterested' criticism — of the appreciation of what Matthew Arnold called 'the best which has been thought and said' (of culture with a capital c) — has fallen foul of a new ideology that declares such things anathema, of a set of values that banishes value.

There is a great deal to be said for these arguments, but in the mouths of many conservative writers they tend to conceal as much as they reveal. For one thing, the anti-PC polemicists tend to write as if 'greatness' is a given, whereas anyone who knows anything about art and culture is aware that this is far from the case. (To take only one of the best-known examples: Shakespeare's reputation as the greatest English playwright was not established until long after his death; in the second half of the 17th century, John Fletcher was considered a superior talent.) Displaying what Michael Berubé describes as a 'libidinal' attachment to the word 'traditional', cultural conservatives are disposed to regard any concession to curricula diversity as a form of positive discrimination, and thus an intolerable attack on 'standards'.[22] And while I take their point about the wholesale politicisation of culture at the hands of the relativists and multiculturalists, the anti-PCers tend to write as if culture is in some sense *detachable* from politics, and that any criticism that goes beyond the realm of pure appreciation is therefore tainted. In his study of how political correctness has 'sabotaged' art, *The Rape of the Masters*, Roger Kimball suggests that it isn't the *substance* of political correctness to which he objects but its tendency to reduce a work of art to a 'prop in a drama not its own'.[23] Yet it is one thing to say that a work's intrinsic value is not reducible to its 'politics', and quite another to claim that its politics are not a proper subject for study. The question is: why are cultural conservatives so in thrall to aesthetic 'detachment'? Could it be that the idea of culture as mutable and subject to radical reassessment constitutes a threat to their political worldview; that all their talk about transcendence and tradition reveals a love for the status quo?

I think it could. Kimball's suggestion that it isn't the substance of political correctness that bothers him is disingenuous, to say the least. Kimball, in common with other conservative critics, has a deep suspicion of the left in general, and his career-defining attacks on political correctness owe almost as much to that suspicion as they do to his desire to defend high culture. Would he have written *Tenured Radicals* if academics had been pumping out papers on the efficacy of traditional family arrangements as revealed in the novels of Jane Austen? Almost certainly not. The problem for Kimball is not just the fact that art has been relegated to 'a prop in a drama'; the problem is the nature of the drama itself — the ideological assumptions underlying it, and the roles it assigns to people like him. The battle between PC and anti-PC is not some arcane academic debate; it is a debate about the nature of society itself, and the right is just as guilty as the left of attempting to use the world of scholarship to press its ideological claims.

Black Armbands and White Blindfolds

Perhaps the most serious allegation made against political correctness is that it can sanction a twisted view of history. As we've seen, there is a tendency for the more extreme multiculturalists to seek to change the history curriculum in order to boost the self-esteem of non-European children and young adults — to turn history, in the words of Diane Ravitch, into a 'tool for group therapy or political action'.[24] But here, again, the right has proven itself both ready and willing to exaggerate the phenomenon when it suits its ideological agenda.

Nowhere is this more apparent than in Australia. Indeed, the Australian 'history wars' are the perfect laboratory to study the way that conservatives take up the anti-PC mantra to push their own ideological vision, adopting a victim mentality in order, so they say, to challenge a history in which the victims have become the heroes, and the heroes, the villains.

The history wars in Australia focus largely on the issue of the country's Indigenous inhabitants. Up until the 1970s, orthodox historians tended to regard Aboriginal people and Torres Strait Islanders as largely peripheral to the national story. No doubt the arrival of Europeans in Australia had not been a happy experience for the natives; but colonial expansion, these historians reasoned, was an inevitable consequence of Western superiority. To deplore it was not only naïve but also pointless. When sophisticated peoples come into contact, or indeed conflict, with unsophisticated ones, the latter must either adapt or die — a fact of nature no less than history.

But in the 1970s this 'natural' process began to be seen in a different light. Revisionist historians started to talk not of settlement but of dispossession. In fact, they began to talk of *invasion*, challenging the traditional narrative of inevitable and beneficent expansion in much the same way that historians in the United States had challenged the cult of Christopher Columbus. Taking their lead from William Stanner, the anthropologist who in 1968 had coined the phrase 'the Great Australian Silence' to describe the way in which Aboriginal people had been effectively erased from Australian history, historians such as Henry Reynolds sought to complicate the historical picture and restore the 'negative facts of history' (Stanner's phrase) to centre stage.[25]

By the 1990s this self-critical emphasis had found its way from the universities into the highest echelons of the political class. In his 1992 Redfern speech, prime minister Paul Keating outlined the horrors that white Australians had visited upon the Indigenous population. In so doing, he gave an enormous boost to the campaign for Aboriginal reconciliation, which sought not only justice and equity but also recognition of Australia's Aboriginal heritage. Meanwhile, the new Australian history also played a crucial role in the campaign for Aboriginal land rights, and the national inquiry into the Stolen Generations in 1997, *Bringing Them Home*, touched off a wave of national soul-searching. Here was the arrogance of Empire writ large — solid evidence, if such were needed, of the injustices at the heart of the Australian experience.

For anyone of a liberal or left persuasion, all these developments were long overdue. But for many conservatives, this revision of history represented nothing less than the wholesale criminalisation of Australia's past. An exercise in political correctness conceived in leftwing universities and promulgated by the publicly funded Australian Broadcasting Corporation, it had undermined Australian pride and corroded Australian unity. It had, in the words of historian Geoffrey Blainey, sanctioned a 'black armband' view of history.[26]

But where Blainey, who coined this picturesque phrase in a speech in 1993, was careful to set the 'black armband' view against what he called the 'three cheers' view and suggest that an unduly positive historiography had given way to an unduly negative one, other conservatives were not so subtle. Certainly John Howard, who became prime minister in March 1996, had little to say about the sins of the past, preferring to berate the new historians for politicising history. For him, politically correct historians had corrupted an otherwise noble discipline. As he put it in a speech in 1996: 'One of the more insidious developments in Australian political life over the past decade or so has been the attempt to rewrite Australian history in the service of a partisan political cause.'[27]

For Howard, who loved to paint himself as the victim of an intolerant PC orthodoxy, the left had robbed Australians of their national self-esteem. By contrast, he hoped to make his countrymen 'relaxed and comfortable' about their past. In particular, he exploited popular sentiment regarding Australia's *military* history, especially its role in World War I. As Stuart MacIntyre has noted, one of the ironies of Howard's approach to the past is that while criticising 'black armband' history and its concomitant invitations to teary self-criticism, he also encouraged a sentimental attitude to Australia's more recent military engagements. It was an audacious strategy, and it worked like a charm: Howard's reign was witness to an explosion of patriotism — an explosion echoed by a rightwing commentariat determined to reverse the damage done to Australia's self-image by the PC left. *The Australian* and the *Quadrant* monthly were only too happy to biff the opposition, which, in timeless rightwing style, they did while affecting to block a punch. Plus they had an ace up the sleeve — or a horseshoe in the glove — in the form of a Sydney-based historian who, having started out on the left, had come to see the error of his ways and was now preparing to atone for them in what can only be described as sensational fashion.

It would be cheap to say that if Keith Windschuttle didn't exist it would be necessary for the Australian right to invent him. It would also be inaccurate. Were the right to invent a history warrior, it couldn't very well do much worse than the man compared by one of his critics to a prosecutor at a Moscow show trial.[28] Nevertheless, this bumptious ex-lefty is central to the conservative backlash against PC; with fanatical application, he has set out to dismantle the 'orthodox school' — as he describes it — of Australian frontier history.[29]

The assault began in the early 1990s. In his 1994 book *The Killing of History*, Windschuttle described the ways in which post-structuralism, identity politics, and political correctness had undermined the discipline of history. Central to this 'mortal attack' was the idea that it is impossible to tell the truth about the past — that we all see history from our own perspective, and that our perspective is what matters in the end. The notion of objective truth had yielded to cultural relativism, the weed of which had taken root not only in US universities but also in Australian ones, where historians of a progressive bent could use the tools of post-structuralism to chip away at 'official' history and construct in its stead a historical narrative more amenable to a leftist worldview. As Windschuttle argued in his introduction, the effect of such an approach to history was to collapse the distinction between history and myth.[30]

Over the next eight years, Windschuttle continued to jab away at the opposition, casting himself as the scourge of the 'elites' (in time-honoured anti-PC fashion) and accusing certain historians ('white activists') of seeking the 'reorganisation and even the eventual break-up of the Australian nation'.[31] But it was only in 2002 that the scale of his ambition became apparent. In that year, he published volume one of *The Fabrication of Aboriginal History*, which argues that leftwing historians in Australia have distorted the nature of European settlement, privileging accounts of frontier conflicts that reinforce their ideological position, and characterising an often complex encounter as a massacre of the innocents. In particular, argues Windschuttle, they have vastly exaggerated the number of Aboriginal deaths at the hands of the European settlers. Mounting guard over this 'genocide thesis', they cover up one another's mistakes and seek to suppress all opinions opposed to their own. Like participants in a rigged séance, all of whom are in on the act, they move the shot glass around the table in accordance with a pre-agreed script.

Windschuttle identifies a number of mistakes in the work of 'orthodox' historians. For example, he claims that Lyndall Ryan, the author of a history of Tasmania's Aborigines, had wilfully misrepresented her sources in an effort to paint the colonial settlers as more violent than they were.[32] Certainly there were some glaring errors in her book, and suggestions that these were honest mistakes fail to explain why all the inaccuracies were, so to say, in one direction. But the accusation of political bias in the work of certain leftwing historians was, for Windschuttle, merely the preamble to a far more radical and far-reaching project: a counter-history in which the Aborigines were not the victims of a genocide at all, but the (admittedly unfortunate) recipients of some sporadic and very limited colonial aggression. For Windschuttle, leftwing historians — veterans of the counterculture, or the heirs to its salient habits of mind — had not just tinkered with the evidence; they'd concocted an entirely imaginary narrative.

And so, against this imaginary narrative Windschuttle set his own account of the interface between the European settlers and Australia's Indigenous peoples, rejecting the interpretive framework employed by earlier historians and suggesting that the colonisation of Australia was carried out with relatively little violence and a conscientious regard for the law. It was, to put it mildly, an audacious analysis, at the heart of which was a radical revision of the statistics regarding Aboriginal deaths at the hands of European settlers. In regard to events in the state of Tasmania, for example, Windschuttle could find 'plausible' evidence of 'only' 118 fatalities.[33]

As Windschuttle's fellow conservative Gerard Henderson pointed out, that 'only' was unfortunate.[34] But more was at issue than Windschuttle's compassion, or rather his conspicuous lack of it. His statistical method was also questionable. In Windschuttle's eyes, a 'plausible' death was one that had been reported upon. Clearly, this was a stringent criterion — so stringent that many commentators regarded it as an attempt to load the dice. As Robert Manne put it in the introduction to *Whitewash*, a collection of analytical essays written in response to *Fabrication*, 'By the use of a methodology equivalent to Windschuttle's it would be possible to prove that virtually no sexual abuse of children occurred in Western societies before the 1970s.'[35] Moreover, Windschuttle, while affecting to remove all speculation from the historical picture, furnished his readers with some pretty colourful, not to say eccentric, speculation of his own. Certainly his suggestion that the colonial authorities would have baulked at killing innocent human beings because Christianity proscribes such behaviour struck many readers as peculiar.[36]

Self-flagellation is an unsightly practice, and many are the non-bigoted Australians who find public apologies for past crimes and other manifestations of white shame both historically illiterate and politically irrelevant; what

French writer Pascal Bruckner calls 'the tyranny of guilt' is one of the pathologies of modern liberalism, unhelpful to the cause of justice and, as I'll argue in the next chapter, ultimately corrosive of it. But what Windschuttle and his spruikers did was to exaggerate the challenge of political correctness in order to advance their own ideology, at the heart of which sits a vision of the West as essentially superior and therefore essentially innocent. In short, in seeking to remove the black armband, they have urged their countrymen to don a white blindfold.

As Manne suggested, Windschuttle was 'singing a song many people wanted to hear', not least John Howard and *The Australian*, in which there appeared a number of editorials favourable to *Fabrication*. (Even Roger Kimball welcomed the book in his magazine *The New Criterion*, calling it 'a scholarly masterpiece'.)[37] Clearly, conservatives were ready for a history that restored some pride to the national conversation. But history, of course, is about facts, not pride. And while a careful questioning of certain assumptions may have been in order, or even overdue, in dismissing so much in so mendacious a way Windschuttle behaved like the kind of historian he attempts to skewer in *The Killing of History*. In that book, he writes that while myth is 'comforting', history is — or should be — 'bracing'. And yet a comforting history was precisely the thing that Howard envisaged for the Australian people, and the thing that his de facto historian-in-chief helped to frame and promulgate. Giving voice to a growing sense of white victimhood, and in common with his fellow US conservatives, Windschuttle used anti–political correctness as the excuse for an ideological land-grab.

Christmas-treeing PC

In the 1980s and 1990s, when political correctness was in its infancy, it was not unusual to hear conservative commentators describe it as the 'McCarthyism of the left'. But if anything bears comparison with McCarthyism, it is the tactics of the anti-PCers. In fact, we could go further and argue that anti-PC, in its most virulent form, is McCarthyism in an eye-catching new outfit — one tailored at precisely the point in history when the old threat was finally laid to rest beneath the rubble of the Berlin Wall. By treating PC as a coherent ideology — an agreed-upon *program* of the cultural left — the right was able to widen its focus from individual instances of political correctness to the liberal 'campaign' against mainstream values and the traditional family with comparative ease. Just as in the 1950s any concession to progressive thinking was deemed to be evidence of communist infiltration, so in the 1980s and 1990s any manifestation of political correctness was seen as proof of a broader project. Nor was this simple paranoia on the right's part; it was a savvy ideological powerplay. The aim of the right was to rout the left while seeming to fight a rearguard action.

This tactic is not confined to universities or to those who write high-end history books; it is also a feature of popular culture. Take, for example, the annual debate about Christmas in the United States, a debate now as redolent of the festive season as mulled wine and chestnut stuffing. Every year, Fox News presenters, shock jocks, and other assorted *enragés* go into a frenzy over 'the war on Christmas', accusing politically correct ideologues of waging a campaign against the traditional holiday in the name of multicultural 'sensitivity' and evangelical secularism. Nativities banned in school foyers; town squares denuded of their traditional pines; shop assistants saying 'happy holidays' — the list of atrocities chills the blood. And the message seems to have found its mark. According to a 2006 poll in the *Chicago Tribune*, 68 per cent of Americans believe there is a war against Christmas.[38]

For US conservatives in particular, 'the war on Christmas' is a template scandal. The *casus belli* is always the same, but the enemy is interchangeable. In the 1920s, Henry Ford declared Christmas to be under attack from Jews, while in the late 1950s the John Birch Society published a pamphlet accusing communists of trying to take 'Christ out of Christmas'.[39] More recently, it has fallen to liberals and progressives to fulfil the role of anti-Santa. Fox presenters such as Bill O'Reilly — a man for whom an offended expression would appear to be a contractual requirement — dedicate entire shows to the liberal war on Christmas, which, they claim, is really a war on traditional, mainstream American values.

One of O'Reilly's principal targets is the American

Civil Liberties Union (ACLU), which he clearly regards as a front organisation for the cabal of progressives, liberals, and leftists who really run the US show. Motivated by a pedantic determination to defend such civil rights and liberties as are guaranteed by the US Constitution, the ACLU has indeed involved itself in a number of disputes over religious imagery or practices in public places — disputes that bear directly on the issue of the separation of church and state. But O'Reilly knows its *real* motivation. As he put it, in a moment of characteristic spleen: 'It's all part of the secular progressive agenda ... if you can get religion out, then you can pass secular progressive programs like legalisation of narcotics, euthanasia, abortion at will, gay marriage.'[40] Nor is O'Reilly the only commentator to claim an anti-Christmas conspiracy. John Gibson, another yammering bust on the payroll of the Fox News Channel, has also been assigned to the case and is, if anything, even more strident in his prosecution of the PC Grinches than the presenter of *The O'Reilly Factor*. His book *The War on Christmas* is an essay in offendedness — an unbroken howl of indignation from a man to whom a terrible truth (and onerous secret) has been vouchsafed: 'The story of this book, the stunning and shocking revelation contained here, is the perversely widespread war on Christmas that we have all seen in our own personal experiences.'[41] The US author Thomas Frank once suggested that indignation is to backlash culture what the guitar solo is to rock music.[42] If that's so, then John Gibson is Jimi Hendrix.

In fact, there is nothing especially 'stunning' or 'shocking' about *The War on Christmas*, apart from its disingenuousness. Wild exaggeration is Gibson's preferred method: 'It's no longer permissible to wish anyone merry Christmas … [L]iterally any sign of Christmas in public can lead to complaints, litigation, angry protest, threats, and bruised feelings.'[43] Well, of course any sign of Christmas can lead to complaints. The question is, does it? And on that the evidence is underwhelming. Focusing on a handful of controversies, which he affects to treat as representative, Gibson is tenacious in his prosecution of the case. 'I began to connect the dots,' he writes, sounding like the paranoid general in Stanley Kubrick's *Dr Strangelove*, 'and discerned the outlines of the conspiracy.'[44] Nor is this 'conspiracy' peculiar to the United States. For example, he notes how in Birmingham, England, 'Christmas has become Winterval'. What he doesn't note is that the term 'Winterval' was used by Birmingham City Council to promote a whole series of winter events (including Christmas) in the late 1990s, and was never intended to replace Christmas but to draw people in to the new city centre. 'Facts are sacred,' said C. P. Scott, owner and editor of the *Manchester Guardian*. Not at the Fox Network they ain't.

Like O'Reilly, Gibson is at pains to stress that the assault on Christmas is really an assault on Christianity and traditional values. To that end, he wilfully misrepresents the ACLU's efforts to preserve church–state separation: 'In all the dramas described here that have played out over bans on the public celebration of Christmas, the plaintiff's reason is always that Christmas is Christian, and symbols of Christianity can't be permitted in public places.'[45] Here, two reasons — 'Christmas is Christian' and 'symbols of Christianity can't be permitted in public places'— are, like a pantomime horse, dressed up as one. The separation of church and state is designed to protect religion from the state as much as it is the state from religion, and the ACLU has often sought to defend the principle of freedom of worship. But here, the insinuation is that the effort to preserve church–state separation is motivated by anti-religious feeling — indeed, that the anti-religious feeling is identical with the constitutional position. A comparable misrepresentation is at work in the description of the union as a 'leftist' organisation; this ignores the many occasions on which the ACLU has defended the rights of neo-Nazis and Ku Klux Klansmen.

Why has the right chosen Christmas as the field on which to battle with the cultural left? The reason is that it affords conservatives the opportunity to attack the left on a number of issues on which it is suspect. Firstly, Christmas is a religious holiday, and conservatives like to paint themselves as the guardians of traditional morality. Secondly, Christmas is a time for the family, the conventional internal arrangements of which are as dear to the conservative heart as an apple pie baked in the shape of Ronald Reagan. And third — and perhaps less obviously — Christmas presents a financial opportunity. 'The Christmas *kulturkampf* is a growth industry in a shrinking economy,' notes Max Blumenthal, 'providing an effective boost for conservative fundraising and a ratings bonanza for right-wing media.'[46] Religion, family, capitalism: the holy trinity of the US right.

Little Blue Pills

'They feel victimised by those they accuse of cultivating victimisation. Deploring hypersensitivity, they are hypersensitive to every slight directed at white men.'[47] So writes Todd Gitlin, referring to the way conservatives pounce upon political correctness in order to advance their own ideology, adopting a victim mentality in the process. Having moved away from its traditional base and embraced the politics of race and gender, the left has ceded ground to the enemy, which is only too happy to cast itself in the role of protector of common sense and guarantor of traditional values. Thus, the identity politics of the left engenders an identity politics of the right, and from the clash of the two a kind of virtual politics of hyperbole and counter-hyperbole emerges. This virtual politics is to actual politics what pornography is to real sex. For what does the culture warrior sell if not a brand of intellectual Viagra — little blue pills of indignation to stiffen the ideological resolve? The passions aroused are artificial, or are based on artificial grievances. But their potency is not to be denied, nor indeed their corrosive effect on the quality of public discourse.

CHAPTER FOUR

Thou Shalt Not Judge

There comes a time when remorse becomes a second offence that adds to the first without cancelling it. Let us inject in others a poison that has long gnawed away at us: shame. A little guilty conscience in Teheran, Riyadh, Karachi, Moscow, Beijing, Havana, Caracas, Algiers, Damascus, Rangoon, Harare, and Khartoum, to mention them alone, would do these governments, and especially their people, a lot of good.

PASCAL BRUCKNER, *THE TYRANNY OF GUILT*

On 20 March 1991, in his penultimate year as Yale University president, Benno Schmidt delivered an address in New York in which he argued that university speech codes were contrary to the spirit of academic life. For Schmidt, the idea that a university could place limits on freedom of thought and expression, which were protected under the First Amendment, was something more than a travesty; it undermined the academy's purpose. 'Freedom of thought must be Yale's central commitment,' said Schmidt, before adding that such a commitment was only meaningful if it extended to thought that 'may deserve our contempt'. 'We may well be moved to exercise our own freedom to counter it or to ignore it. But universities cannot censor or suppress speech, no matter how obnoxious in content, without violating their justification for existence.'

Turning to the beliefs underpinning the speech codes, Yale's head honcho continued:

> On some other campuses in this country, values of civility and community have been offered by some as paramount values of the university, even to the extent of superseding freedom of expression.
>
> Such a view is wrong in principle and, if extended, is disastrous to freedom of thought ... The chilling effects on speech of the vagueness and open-ended nature of many universities' prohibitions ... are compounded by the fact that these codes are typically enforced by faculty and students who commonly assert that vague notions of community are more important to the academy than freedom of thought and expression.[1]

Thus Schmidt characterised the conflict between speech codes and free speech as a clash of values. As he put it, a little portentously, 'This is a flabby and uncertain time for freedom in the United States.'

More than 20 years after Schmidt's peroration, the value of free speech is looking no less flabby and no more certain of its place in the world; indeed, if anything, its waistband has expanded and its indecision attained to senility. Take for example the statement from the director of Yale University Press (YUP), John Donatich, on the Press's decision not to publish the infamous Muhammad caricatures in Jytte Klausen's 2009 book, *The Cartoons That Shook the World*, a meticulous if at times wrongheaded account of the saturnalia of violence and self-pity that was the Danish cartoons controversy:

> Would including the illustrations enhance the book? The easy answer is, of course, yes. But the book's reader will quickly discover that it is not a graphic analysis of the cartoons or a history of depictions of the Prophet Muhammad. Rather, it is an intrepid detective story that investigates the nature and source of the protests that followed the publication of the Danish cartoons …
>
> And the cartoons are deliberately grotesque and insulting, gratuitously so. They were designed to pick a fight. They meant to hurt and provoke. At best, they are in bad taste. The press would never have commissioned or published them as original content … And finally, there was an argument to be made that printing the cartoons and accompanying illustrations would simply perpetuate the misunderstandings and reignite the very conflict that it intends to analyze in a balanced and nuanced way …
>
> We knew from Klausen's own chronology that the original publication in 2005 of the cartoons by the Danish newspaper led to a series of violent incidents worldwide and over 200 deaths. Republication of the cartoons has

repeatedly resulted in violence …

In the end, I decided that the press would omit the images, knowing that this was the kind of decision that could not be made without negative consequences. Many people feel that my choice was impolitic or politically incorrect [*sic*] or just plain wrong. Yet I believe it was the responsible, principled, practical, and right thing to do …

Klausen's book will now appear at the end of this month [September], rather than in November as originally scheduled … Our hope is that its appearance will clarify the issues and further engage the debate.[2]

Well, it certainly engaged the debate, though not quite in the way that the author would have wanted. The decision not to print the Muhammad caricatures transformed Klausen's book from an analysis of the cartoons controversy into a depressing (though telling) coda to it. Like a news photographer at a demonstration suddenly swept up and along by the crowd, the Norwegian professor entered the story in a way she'd neither desired nor anticipated.

For what struck many about YUP's decision, which was taken against the author's wishes and which came to dominate discussion of her book, was the conspicuous mixing of registers. If Donatich had said that he took the decision on the basis of security considerations alone, few could have questioned his reasoning, even if such a capitulation looked like a case of crying before hurt. But that is not what Donatich said. Rather, he attempted to give his decision a veneer of moral integrity by focusing on the 'insulting' character of the cartoons: 'They were designed to pick a fight. They meant to hurt and provoke. At best, they are in bad taste.' Well, some of them are and some of them aren't, but that is hardly the point, is it? For what Donatich declines to say is whether he'd be willing to risk his own life and the lives of his colleagues for some other cartoons — cartoons he deemed in better taste, though no less insulting to a section of the community. And if he would, was he saying that the protesters laying waste to European embassies had a point?

Donatich's evident confusion on this issue (was he claiming the moral high ground or merely taking cover?) is typical of the phenomenon of self-censorship, where the language of 'sensitivity' is pressed into service to conceal simple fear. What we find in many of these debates are two kinds of offence-taking working in concert: on the one hand, we have the hurt feelings of the faithful, some of whom claim the God-given right to murder those who would question their beliefs; and on the other, we have the (vicarious) offendedness of those schooled in the multiculturalist ethos of difference and non-judgementalism. The trouble is that this non-judgementalism appears to extend to the fanatically judgemental. Not to the Ku Klux Klan, of course, nor to the Westboro Baptists. But for anyone whose skin is on the dark side, the apologies — implicit or explicit — are forthcoming. I don't want to overstate the case; I'm sure Mr

Donatich was appalled by certain Muslims' reactions to the Danish cartoons. But the fact remains that in his long and careful statement he strenuously condemns the caricatures but not the violence attendant upon their publication. Nor does he have a word to say about the value of freedom of speech and expression, and the difficult and demanding principle at its core, without which it is simply an empty piety.

Voltaire didn't ever actually state the aphorism attributed to him: 'I disapprove of what you say but will defend to the death your right to say it.' But someone did, and whoever it was put his or her finger on a fundamental principle — a principle reiterated by Benno Schmidt in New York in 1991. The Yale alumnus surveyed the university campus and saw that that principle was under attack from a different set of priorities, and, nearly 20 years later, the publishing arm of his own university confirmed his prescience, as did many other publishers and media outlets across the West. A failure of nerve and of principle, this capitulation to the forces of reaction was all the more depressing for being unsurprising. How we got to *that* stage is what we'll explore in this chapter.

Rushdie Redux

So let's recap. On 30 September 2005, the Danish newspaper *Jyllands-Posten* published a handful of rather second-rate cartoons depicting the Islamic prophet Muhammad. The caricatures were inspired by the case of

Kåre Bluitgen, a children's author who, it's claimed, had had problems finding an illustrator for his biography of the Prophet, the depiction of whom is prohibited by certain hadith. To the newspaper's culture editor, Flemming Rose, Bluitgen's failure to secure an artist was revealing of an atmosphere of fear and self-censorship. He invited 40 cartoonists to send in drawings of Muhammad, 12 of which he subsequently printed. (One shows Muhammad with a bomb-shaped turban, while another shows him at the gates of heaven addressing a group of suicide bombers: 'Stop! Stop! We've run out of virgins!')

Four months later, the paper had been inundated with expressions of grief and anger from Muslims, Danish imams having spared no effort in hawking the cartoons around the Middle East in an attempt to get diplomatic backing for their campaign against *Jyllands-Posten*. A number of countries had launched a trade boycott of Danish goods, and Danish consulates and embassies had been torched. Around 200 people died in the protests. As journalist Henryk Broder put it in German news magazine *Der Spiegel*, it was 'as though a second Abu Ghraib had been discovered in a suburb of Copenhagen'.[3]

Early on in the cartoons crisis, it became obvious that offence was being utilised by groups and governments eager to press their own agendas or gain political leverage, or simply divert attention away from their own economic or administrative failings. In Pakistan, the religious party Jamaat-e-Islami used the crisis as a tool to apply pressure to the president, Pervez Musharraf, perceived by many religious Pakistanis to be far too friendly with the United States. Similarly, in Indonesia the extremist Islamic Defenders Front used the controversy as an opportunity to excite popular feeling against the West, attempting to storm the Danish embassy in Jakarta beneath placards reading 'Let's slaughter the Danish ambassador'. Nor was it only religious parties that attempted to weaponise the crisis. The Ba'athist government in Syria used it to consolidate its power at home — by giving the nod to a protest in Damascus that led to the burning of the Danish and Norwegian embassies — and in neighbouring Lebanon, where its agents bussed in protesters bent on anti-Christian violence.

This is not to say that the cartoons crisis was entirely orchestrated. In order for these groups and governments to exploit religious indignation, there had to be religion in place, and any account of the cartoons crisis which fails to take account of *that* is no account at all. Not that it's hard to analyse; the protesters were merely fulfilling a prophecy set down not in but *by* sacred books: namely, that those who adhere to them will take offence when those books are rejected, or mocked, or otherwise called into question. From Torquemada's hot-blooded enforcers to the Birmingham rioters of 1791, history is replete with examples of this, and the future will be replete with them too. There is very little mystery about it. It comes, as they say, with the territory.

In one sense, then, the offence that was taken at the Danish cartoons was entirely straightforward: it was the rage of the faithful against the infidel, a rage whipped up and weaponised by demagogues across the 'Islamic' world. Attempts by various liberal commentators to reduce the anti-cartoons protests to a *cri de coeur* from an oppressed community were as overstated as they were predictable. The publication of 12 cartoons, and not the so-called war on terror or the United States' support for Israel, was the issue on which the protests centred. Yes, the US flag was burned and the US president denounced as a Zionist. But the central issue was blasphemy, not bombs. 'Butcher those who mock Islam' and 'Freedom go to hell' read two of the placards at a demonstration in central London. It doesn't get much clearer than that.

But there *was* something else going on, especially in the Western context, where it was plain that some protesters saw themselves not just as divinely privileged but also as abnormally victimised. At once the beneficiaries of God's grace and the sufferers of a bitter injustice, their mood seemed pitched between self-righteousness and self-pity. At some level, a proud religious boast had fused with a narrative of victimisation.

Of course, we'd seen all this before — 16 years before, to be exact, when Iran's supreme leader Ayatollah Khomeini sought to place himself at the head of a campaign against an award-winning magical-realist novel by sentencing its author, Salman Rushdie, to death. The *Satanic Verses* controversy was both the forerunner to and template for the Danish cartoons crisis; anybody who in February 2006 didn't think immediately of February 1989 simply hadn't been paying attention.

Let's not revisit the events surrounding the Rushdie affair; they have been written about many times before, most recently by Rushdie himself, in his massive memoir *Joseph Anton*. Suffice it to say that the same combination of popular religious indignation and localised political opportunism at work in the cartoons controversy was also at work in the earlier crisis. But one aspect of the Rushdie controversy does demand re-emphasis, and that is the spectacular and (ostensibly) sudden way in which an old form of offence-taking — the religious form — fused seamlessly with a newer phenomenon, namely identity politics. It is here, in the amalgamation of two kinds of sensitivity, that one of the most interesting and important aspects of modern indignation comes into focus.

In his peerless study of the causes and consequences of the Rushdie affair, *From Fatwa to Jihad*, the British journalist Kenan Malik puts this development into historical context. For him, it is inextricably bound up with the policy of multiculturalism outlined in 1966 by the then British home secretary and Labour MP Roy Jenkins.[4] In contrast to the strategy of national and cultural assimilation by which immigrants were absorbed into the dominant culture, Jenkins envisaged an enlightened era of 'cultural diversity, coupled with equal opportunity, in an atmosphere of mutual tolerance'. While such sentiments seem unremarkable today (if anything, phrases such as 'cultural diversity' come rather too trippingly off the political tongue), in the United Kingdom in the mid 1960s they stood out against the national conversation like a tie-dye shirt in a gentlemen's club. The 'flattening process of uniformity', as Jenkins described it, was no longer hip; according to him, the British should recognise and celebrate difference.

The policy sounded — and still sounds — decent, but it had an unintended consequence: over time, it led to a situation in which certain ethnic minority communities became separated from the 'mainstream' culture. Of course, it wasn't the only factor that led to this development. There were also the dynamics of 'chain migration', by which early settlers encouraged others, especially friends and family members, to follow them into the same communities; and, of course, there was the galvanising effect on immigrant populations of native racial prejudice. But the policy of multiculturalism added something new to the mix. Encouraging a more 'hands-off' attitude to minority cultures and value systems, it helped to bring about a state of affairs in which Jenkins' prediction of 'mutual tolerance' began to sound more than a little hollow.

For Malik, the son of Muslim immigrants who settled in northern England in the 1960s, Jenkins' comments were an early symptom that progressives were turning away from universalism — from the leftwing notion that 'we're all in this together' — and towards the essentialist politics of identity. In the past, he writes, to be on the left was to be secular and internationalist. Of course, the black community faced issues the white community didn't have to. But when it came to fundamental values such as rights for women and economic justice, radicals from both communities recognised their mutual interests — and, indeed, their mutual enemies. Yet by the early 1980s, as the left took its leave of traditional class politics, choosing instead to refocus its attention on issues of race and sexuality, immigrants looked around for other causes through which to voice their disaffection. Taking refuge in cultural identity, they insisted on difference and separation; solidarity *between* different oppressed groups shrank to solidarity *within* them.

Nowhere is this more apparent than in Britain's diverse Asian community, in which extremist Islam now furnishes some young Muslims with what Malik, following Turkish-French sociologist Nilüfer Göle, calls an 'affirmative reconstruction of identity'.[5] Expressive of both authenticity and difference, Islamism in this manifestation is less a demonstration of religious devotion than a species of identity politics. It is no coincidence that radical groups such as Hizb ut-Tahrir, which agitates for Sharia law and the restoration of the Islamic Caliphate, began organising on university campuses in the late 1980s and the 1990s: with the traditional left in full retreat from the forces of neoliberalism, and identity politics in its ascendant phase, the time was ripe for just such a development. And needless to say, the Rushdie affair served as a convenient *casus belli* for those young, disaffected Muslims who proved amenable to such approaches. Linking arms with the very mullahs to whom, as secular internationalists, they wouldn't have given the time of day, they took to the streets in Bradford and London and burned the work of a fellow immigrant who, incidentally, had never ceased to campaign for racial equality and justice. In so doing, they sent an unambiguous message that the political arrangements of yesteryear were no longer relevant to many British Muslims. Like black nationalists in the United States, they would eschew integration and embrace segregation, albeit segregation on their own terms. In one sense, the old black radical slogan 'self-defence is no offence' — pressed into service whenever minorities fought back against their racist tormentors — was inverted during the course of the Rushdie affair. It now read 'offence is self-defence'.

To this extent, 1989 really did point forward to 2006. In Denmark, there were issues underlying the cartoons controversy that may not have been immediately apparent to spectators outside the country: an increasingly acrimonious and demagogic debate about immigration; a rise in anti-Islamic bigotry; and a sense, not entirely unjustified, that Muslims in general were being blamed for the actions of al-Qaeda and other fringe movements. Those issues deserved a proper airing. But you cannot fight reactionary positions with even more reactionary positions any more than you can fight fire with paraffin, and the position of the anti-cartoons protesters, a combination of identity politics and religious intolerance, was deeply reactionary. Fundamentally, it rested on two forms of offence-taking: one deriving from wrongheaded ideas of racial and cultural essentialism, and one deriving from holy writ. And its effect was to drown the genuine grievances the Muslim community had — and has — in such a wail of misdirected piety as would drown out the most enthusiastic muezzin.

Don't Mention the War

If the policy of multiculturalism is partly responsible for the disengagement of immigrant communities, it is also partly responsible for the inability of politicians and others to deal effectively with violent outbreaks such as the Danish cartoons crisis. Again, the issue is not straightforward. Often, the reason publishers and others back down in the face of intimidation is that they are, to put it bluntly, scared. But concern for racial or religious sensibilities also has its part to play; and while the language of 'offence', 'respect', and 'sensitivity' can give an act of fearfulness the look of something more high-minded, it is also clear that those who employ it often do so with complete sincerity. For them, the argument that freedom of speech must include the freedom to offend fails to take account of the fact that often the person doing the offending is a lot more powerful than the person being offended.

In some ways, it's a noble argument — or at least an argument that comes from a noble place. But it leads the advocate into immediate difficulties, including moral evasion in the face of intransigence. Time and again in the months after the cartoons crisis, commentators of a liberal persuasion sought to lay the blame for the chaos at the door of the newspaper that had published the cartoons, rather than with the protesters wreaking havoc or the politicians egging them on. They pointed out that *Jyllands-Posten's* stunt was revealing of anti-Islamic sentiment not just among Denmark's political class but also within the European community. All of which was well worth saying, as long as those saying it remained clear on the main point — namely, that having your feelings hurt doesn't give you the right to riot or violate diplomatic immunity or attack Scandinavian nationals living in the Middle East. Too often, liberal sympathy for Muslims facing intolerance in Western societies shaded into exculpation of Muslim protesters everywhere. At the very least, there was a marked inability to understand precisely what was at stake. When, for example, a handful of European newspapers chose to reproduce the cartoons in solidarity with *Jyllands-Posten*, they were roundly criticised by politicians and commentators, including the British foreign minister Jack Straw, for their insensitivity and irresponsibility. How could these papers risk more death and destruction for the sake of a few mediocre cartoons — cartoons that were, in John Donatich's words, 'grotesque and insulting, gratuitously so'? But in reproducing the cartoons, these papers weren't endorsing their content; rather, they were mounting guard over a principle. That so few media outlets followed suit was not only a scandal in itself; it also raised the possibility that any group with an axe to grind could intimidate the press in the future.

This anxiety found an official outlet in a report by the UN's Commission on Human Rights, which was deeply critical of the Danish government's handling of the cartoons crisis. 'Politically and from the standpoint of the morality of international relations,' it stated,

> the Danish Government, against the backdrop of an alarming resurgence of defamation of religions, especially Islamophobia but also anti-Semitism and Christianophobia, failed to show the commitment and vigilance that it normally displays in combating religious intolerance and incitement to religious hatred and promoting religious harmony.[6]

According to the author of the report, Doudou Diène, United Nations special rapporteur on contemporary forms of racism, both the Danish government's failure to adopt an official stance on the content of the cartoons and its subsequent refusal to grant an audience to ambassadors from Muslim countries whose stated aim was to urge the prime minister, Anders Fogh Rasmussen, to censor his own press — a thing he was simply not able to do, even if he'd wanted to — were *themselves* revealing of anti-Islamic prejudice.

'The initial reaction of the Danish government,' he opined, 'revealed not just the trivialization of Islamophobia at the political level but also, as events subsequently demonstrated, the central involvement of politicians in the national and international impact of manifestations and expressions of Islamophobia.'[7] Apparently, anyone who stuck up for free speech in the face of violence and intimidation was now guilty of religious discrimination.

Where does this pusillanimity come from? It comes, surely, from the very blending of religion and identity politics that fuelled the cartoons crisis in the first place. The portmanteau word 'Islamophobia' is revealing in this regard. Combining a religion ('Islam') with the charge of irrational fear ('phobia'), it neatly conflates determined criticism of a set of beliefs and unthinking bigotry. And while much of the criticism of Islam and Muslims *is* akin to unthinking bigotry (and aggravated by racial prejudice), it's as well to keep the two things separate, in principle at any rate, if we don't want to end up in a situation where honest criticism becomes impossible.

To say that the last ten years or so have seen some notable failures in this regard is to put it delicately. On many occasions, Western governments, faced with a conflict between free speech and religion (or some other special-interest group) have managed either to fudge the issue or take the wrong course of action. A case in point is the British government's response to complaints from the Muslim community that the country's ancient blasphemy laws only applied to Christianity. Rather than do the sensible thing and consign the blasphemy laws to the dustbin, the government, led by the devout Tony Blair, proposed to extend them to all religions. Eventually the British House of Lords managed to tone down the legislation, but the *Racial and Religious Hatred Act 2006* is still a defeat for the principle that freedom of speech is meaningless unless it includes the freedom to offend.

This wilful confusion of identity and belief has had a calamitous influence on public policy and on the quality of public discourse. Once you resolve to treat a religion, or any set of beliefs, as an identity, you begin to shield it against criticism and even to discourage objective analysis. If, like me, you believe that criticism is the one thing all religions need, this presents a major problem. For example, if I said that *all* religions are predisposed to intolerance I don't suppose I'd raise many eyebrows, even though some people would disagree with me. But if I were to say that Islam and Islamic extremism exist on a continuum — the same point but in different language — I'd run the risk of serious censure. That Islamic terrorists are motivated by a literal reading of the Qur'an and the Hadith should be an uncontroversial point, and yet politicians and public officials will go to the most extraordinary lengths to avoid the bleeding obvious. One of the most ridiculous episodes in the British government's recent past — in a strong field — was its publication in 2008 of a Home Office counterterrorism phrasebook for civil servants, which proscribed the use of phrases such as 'Islamist extremism' when talking about *Islamist extremism* for fear of giving offence to Muslims.[8] In the same year, the US State Department instructed its employees to avoid such terms as 'jihadist', 'salafi', 'caliphate', and 'wahhabist'; and in 2009, Janet Napolitano, the US secretary of Homeland Security, eschewed the term 'Islamic terrorism' in favour of 'man-made disasters'.[9] Such 'sensitivity' is both condescending — in its implication that ordinary Muslims are unable to distinguish between a description of reality and an attack on their religion — and detrimental to public discourse. As Ed Stourton suggests in *It's a PC World*, trying to talk about Islamic terrorism without referring to the Islamic religion 'is a little like trying to understand the Inquisition, the Crusades and all the burnings and beheadings which disfigured Europe during the sixteenth and seventeenth centuries while pretending that none of them had anything to do with Christianity'.[10]

The Ideological Stroop Effect

Responding to criticism of the counterterrorism phrase-book, a Home Office spokeswoman said that the document had nothing to do with political correctness. Needless to say, she was talking through her hat. The inflated notions of rights and respect, skewed ideas of injury and injustice, and obsession with language revealed in its pages are the direct descendants of political correctness. The concept of cultural relativism has led to an intellectual atmosphere in which commentators are often reluctant to suggest that individual members of an ethnic minority, or indeed a religious minority, may be bigots, or extremists, or worse. As Frank Furedi puts it *On Tolerance*, 'Thou shalt not judge' is now the 'eleventh commandment'.[11]

The problem is that in suspending judgement and opening up your mind to 'difference', you can find yourself apologising for the most closed-minded people on the planet. This was Allan Bloom's point in *The Closing of the American Mind*, and it leads to some obvious difficulties. In a sort of ideological version of the phenomenon known as the Stroop effect, in which the regions of the brain that recognise words interfere with those regions that recognise colour, the left's traditional anti-clericalism has bumped up against identity politics, with the result that the latter has come out on top. As we saw in Chapter Two, this phenomenon is traceable to the disappearance of the 1960s left into the universities, where a politics of 'difference' came to replace an emphasis on class and social justice. This led to a form of multiculturalism in which movements in other parts of the world were regarded as wonderfully exotic and not to be judged or analysed. Suddenly, to criticise other cultures was to be guilty of a kind of cultural imperialism. As the British journalist Nick Cohen puts it,

> If the dictatorial leaders of a foreign state or radical movement, or the usually unelected leaders of a 'community' or religious group said that their culture demanded the

oppression of women and homosexuals, for example, twenty-first century liberals were tripped over by the thought that it was racist to oppose them.

The flip side of this 'debased coinage', argues Cohen, is that democrats, feminists, and socialists in the poor world get no support from their Western 'comrades'.[12]

What we've seen, in short, is the notion of tolerance become hopelessly confused with the notion of acceptance. While tolerance should mean agreeing to disagree, and agreeing on rules about *how* to disagree, acceptance is really a species of indifference. The distinction between the two hinges on the difference between what one *is* and what one *believes*. As a non-racist, I don't *tolerate* Asian people; rather, I *accept* them as equal human beings who happen to come from a different part of the world and whose skin colour happens to differ from mine. Conversely, as someone who dislikes religion, I *tolerate* Islam but I don't *accept* it, any more than I accept Judaism or Christianity, or any other claim to ultimate truth. Confusion on this simple point may stem, as Stefan Collini has argued, from a well-meaning condescension towards minorities.[13] But it leads, in short order, to what Pascal Bruckner has termed a 'rhetoric of expiation'.[14]

Comforting the Afflicted

The ideological Stroop effect is never as conspicuous as in the interface between Islam and women's rights.

Historically, leftwingers could be relied upon to stick up for the principle of sexual equality even if their personal behaviour didn't always live up to their political rhetoric. But faced with conservative Islam, and saddled with a political outlook that discourages any criticism of minorities, the left is led into all kinds of confusion. There's no better demonstration of the fact that cultural relativism is not just *incompatible* with social justice but also ultimately *antithetical* to it.

The confusion is perfectly caught in the left's ambiguous and fraught relationship with certain 'Muslim' intellectuals. Take, for example, the Somali-born activist and polemicist Ayaan Hirsi Ali. Brought up in an Islamic family, subjected to genital mutilation, and threatened with marriage to a distant cousin, Hirsi Ali escaped to the Netherlands in 1992. Since then she has become a ferocious critic of political and non-political Islam, and a lightning rod for religious hatred. Her script for *Submission*, a low-budget film dealing with misogyny in conservative Islam, marked the beginning of this high-profile apostasy: in 2004, the film's director, Theo van Gogh, was murdered in an Amsterdam street; pinned to his ritually mutilated body was a note informing Hirsi Ali to expect a similarly bloody end.

It is generally agreed on the left — or, at any rate, it used to be — that the sexual and economic liberation of women is not just a desirable end in itself but also one of the most important issues facing the developing world. To give women control over their reproductive systems and greater economic independence is the most effective way to fight poverty and lift the living standards of entire populations. And here is a woman, Hirsi Ali, determined to attest to the most spectacular misogyny in large parts of the Islamic world, and to do so at considerable risk to herself. That alone, you might have thought, would have been enough to secure her the respect, if not the unconditional support, of the great majority of those on the left. And yet many liberals appear to regard her as a sort of 'useful idiot' of the anti-immigration right and of those who seek to spin the wars in Iraq and Afghanistan as a moral crusade. 'Ayaan Hirsi Ali has brains and beauty and is a gift to those of us who like our prejudices confirmed,' wrote the Australian journalist Hilary McPhee in her review of Hirsi Ali's memoir *Nomad*, while American journalist Nicholas Kristof, in a piece on the same book, managed to imply that its (death-threatened) author was consciously trying to stir up trouble. Even British historian Timothy Garton Ash, usually a font of liberal good sense, called her an 'Enlightenment fundamentalist' (a shady moral equivalence) and suggested that her views on Islam fell all the more easily on the public's ear for the fact that she was so easy on the eye: 'It's no disrespect to Ms Hirsi Ali to suggest that if she had been short, squat and squinting, her story and views might not be so closely attended to.'[15]

Tellingly, the same liberals who criticise Hirsi Ali are often impressed, inordinately so, with the Muslim writer Tariq Ramadan, a professor of Islamic studies at Oxford

University and the grandson of Hassan al-Banna, the founder of the Muslim Brotherhood. The contrast between the two figures is instructive. While Hirsi Ali is sometimes described (rather exaggeratedly) as an African Voltaire, Ramadan, who describes himself as 'Swiss by nationality, Egyptian by memory, Muslim by religion, European by culture, universalistic by principle [and] Moroccan and Mauritian by adoption',[16] has always been a little more nuanced when it comes to the interface between Islamic doctrine and (so-called) Enlightenment values. In fact, nuance is his metier. Challenged by Nicolas Sarkozy to condemn the practice of stoning for adultery, Ramadan recommended a 'moratorium'.[17] Or here he is describing his method — a postmodern slant on a premodern theology:

(1) There are indeed texts (one verse, and hence some Prophetic traditions) that refer to striking one's wife: I quote them because Muslims read and quote those texts. (2) Here are the interpretations that have been suggested, from the most literalist, which justify striking women in the name of the Quran, to the most reformist, which read this verse in light of the global message and contextualise the verse and Prophetic traditions as well as taking their chronology into account. (3) In light of those interpretations and considering the example set by the Prophet, who never struck a woman, I say that domestic violence contradicts Islamic teachings and that such behaviour must be condemned.[18]

As I wrote in a review of *What I Believe* — the book from which this passage is taken — if you need to go around this many houses in order to conclude that punching your wife is an affront to human decency, perhaps your map is out of date.

Why would any liberal be impressed by such intellectual contortions? Possibly because they've assimilated the view advanced by American humourist Finley Peter Dunne that it is the job of the writer to comfort the afflicted and to afflict the comfortable. The trouble is it isn't always clear who the afflicted and the comfortable *are*. Many are the Muslims who feel wronged by the West, but what about the imbalance of power *within* Muslim-majority countries? Faced with misogyny in the Islamic world, do we argue for more rights for women, even at the risk of appearing to criticise Islam? Or do we take the relativist view that, when it comes to other cultures, it isn't for us in the West to judge? Referring to the many discussions she had about women's rights in Saudi Arabia, American political activist Barbara Ehrenreich puts the dilemma crisply: 'One of the positions was that you can't criticise gender relations in Saudi Arabia, because that's "their" culture. But I'm not comfortable with a political outlook that says I can't criticise what looks to me like gender apartheid.'[19] If only all feminists were as unambiguous. Alas, even the veteran feminist Germaine Greer declines to condemn the practice of female genital mutilation, on the grounds that to do so would reinforce notions of Western cultural superiority.

(In a recent discussion on Australian television, she even drew a facile comparison between genital mutilation and elective labiaplasty.)[20] Thus does the doctrine of cultural relativism undermine the cause of justice.

Identity Pens

In her dystopian novel *The Handmaid's Tale*, Margaret Atwood imagines a future in which the United States, now renamed Gilead, has fallen under the control of Christian fundamentalists. Women are dominated by men, none more so than the eponymous Handmaids, whose job it is to have sexual intercourse with, and bear the children of, the party bigwigs. These Handmaids are required to dress in red habits, with stiff white wings around the head to prevent them from being seen by men — a Christianised version of the dress code imposed on women in some parts of the Muslim world.

In a fictional lecture at the end of the novel — delivered, we are told, at the Twelfth Symposium on Gileadean Studies in Nunavit, Canada — Professor James Darcy Pieixoto reveals that the action of *The Handmaid's Tale* derives from an audio diary kept by its protagonist. Before expanding on the diary's contents, the professor makes the following comment:

> If I may be permitted an editorial aside, allow me to say that in my opinion we must be cautious about passing moral judgment upon the Gileadeans. Surely we have learned by

now that such judgments are of necessity culture-specific. Also, Gileadean society was under a good deal of pressure, demographic and otherwise, and was subject to factors from which we ourselves are happily more free. Our job is not to censure but to understand. (*Applause.*)[21]

Although this passage is heavily satirical, it is precisely the moral dodge advanced by those who decline to criticise societies in which groups such as women are discriminated against. Pieixoto's attitude to a dead society is no different, in the final analysis, to Greer's attitude to certain living ones. The rhetoric sounds respectful, sensitive, and inoffensive, but in essence it's a kind of moral isolationism.

Such isolationism has some dire consequences, perhaps the most egregious of which is the creation of cultural, racial, or religious enclaves within Western societies. The problem with identity politics is that it tends to define people by one characteristic and pre-judge their interests as necessarily influenced or defined by that characteristic. The effect is to confine individual humans to what Kenan Malik has called 'identity pens'.[22] Instead of multiculturalism, we get plural monoculturalism, a society in which respect is accorded not to individuals but to groups of individuals.[23] Thus the 'gated communities of the mind' (as described by Collini) engendered by political correctness become *actual* communities — maybe not gated, but cut off from the mainstream, subject to their own regulations.[24]

At its worst, this produces a situation in which people from ethnic or religious minorities are censored or intimidated by other forces from within the same minority group. In recent years, the United Kingdom has witnessed a number of depressing controversies in which this sort of dynamic is apparent. Take the controversy over British Sikh writer Gurpreet Kaur Bhatti's 2004 play *Behzti*. Bhatti wrote the play (the title of which means 'dishonour' in Punjabi) in order to expose hypocrisy within the Sikh religion and community; she included a confronting scene, set in a Sikh temple, in which a religious elder rapes the female protagonist and is murdered by the protagonist's mother. This proved too much for many British Sikhs, and on 18 December 2004 the Birmingham Repertory Theatre (or 'Rep') was forced to cancel the opening-night performance after protesters attempted to storm the venue, clashing with riot police and prompting the evacuation of some 800 patrons. Two days later, and after intensive talks with representatives from the Sikh community and the West Midlands police, the Rep decided to cancel the play altogether. Bhatti, having received death threats, was temporarily forced into hiding.

'It was not the substance or message of her play that invoked the wrath of so many Sikhs,' wrote Jasdev Singh Rai, the director of the Sikh Human Rights Group, in *The Guardian*, 'but the deliberate, sensational and offensive use of sacred icons.'[25] Similarly, it wasn't the 'substance' of the play that the people who objected to its cancellation were concerned with, but the principle of freedom of expression. Yet while Rai provided chapter and verse in defence of his opposition to the play (as well as a few revealing references to postmodern gurus such as Michel Foucault), the British government's defence of free speech was timorous, to say the least. Fiona Mactaggart, the under-secretary of state with responsibility for criminal justice, race equality, and communities, seemed strangely reluctant to condemn the violence, while the arts minister, Estelle Morris, said that although the closure of the play represented a 'sad day for freedom of speech', the Rep had nevertheless done 'the right thing' by the staff and actors for whom it was responsible. Needless to say, there were many actors — and writers and artists — who disagreed with the minister and who despaired of her weak response to the crisis.[26]

Such official timidity was again in evidence in July 2006, when Sylhet Bangladeshis took objection to the filming of Monica Ali's *Brick Lane*, a novel about a Bangladeshi woman sent to London to be married off to a man old enough to be her father. Ruby Films had originally intended to shoot the film in Brick Lane itself, but residents of the narrow street in East London sometimes known as 'Banglatown' took offence at the novel's portrayal of Bangladeshis. Acting on police advice, the film company moved its operations elsewhere. Not that this satisfied all of the protesters; emboldened by the smell of blood in their nostrils, many continued to campaign against the film, at several points predicting violence should shooting go ahead.

That Ruby Films felt compelled to move from its preferred location was bad enough. But that the British government did not see fit to take a principled stand on the issue was nothing less than a national disgrace. In a statement, the writers' union English PEN lamented the lack of political and police support: 'English PEN believes that community censorship unopposed by the state is effectively state censorship by proxy.'[27]

Not everyone agreed. Unimpressed by the argument that the source of Bangladeshi offence had less to do with racial stereotyping than with Ali's depiction of a young Muslim woman engaged in a sexual mutiny against her husband, Germaine Greer (her again) went into print with a defence of the anti–*Brick Lane* protesters. According to Greer, they had the 'moral right' to drive the cameras out of Brick Lane. Moreover, Ali was a cultural impostor. 'She writes in English and her point of view is, whether she allows herself to impersonate a village Bangladeshi woman or not, British.'[28] As Salman Rushdie pointed out, Greer's position smacked of 'double racism': 'To suit Germaine Greer, the British-Bangladeshi Ali is denied her heritage and belittled for her Britishness, while her British-Bangladeshi critics are denied that same Britishness, which most of them would certainly insist was theirs by right.'[29] Rushdie hit the nail on the head. In attempting to 'essentialise' two communities — the one 'British', the other 'Bangladeshi' — Greer inadvertently demonstrated the shallowness of cultural relativism. Indeed, she made the same mistake as those Western governments who attempt to communicate with their minority populations through community 'leaders'; the mistake is to forget that no culture is uniform and that such leaders are often unrepresentative. (In the case of the anti-*Brick Lane* protests, 'the community' turned out to be nothing more than a group of local businessmen backed by a bit of local muscle.) And the result of that mistake is a big step backwards — to a situation in which religious communities could pronounce anathema on 'one of their own'. To anyone committed to the ideals of the Enlightenment, that should be a cause for consternation.

Identity and Racism

Greer's comments on the *Brick Lane* controversy also highlight another problem with the politics of identity — the way in which it *encourages* racism. This may sound like a counterintuitive statement; after all, it was in order to challenge racist attitudes that identity politics got going in the first place. But my point is not to impugn the motives of those who flirt with cultural relativism. Rather, it is to stress the way in which relativism both sanctions racist attitudes (albeit in a tangential way) and causes the left to desert such fields as the far right is only too happy to occupy.

To reiterate, the 'defining error' of identity politics, according to Collini, is to assume that people's interests and needs are reducible to their race, religion, or ethnicity.[30] This mirrors the very racist attitudes it is supposed to counteract. Referring to the guidelines on bias employed by US textbook publishers and state education agencies, Diane Ravitch writes, 'These are people who look at others and see not an individual but a person who represents a group ... Ordinarily, in the world of bias guidelines, the identification of the individual with the characteristics of a group is considered stereotyping.'[31] The relevance of this to the political sphere is, or ought to be, self-evident. Those who would urge us not to pass judgement on other cultures *on account of their otherness* are themselves engaging in stereotyping behaviour.

Moreover, by insulating communities in this way, the defenders of cultural relativism are apt to find themselves turning a blind eye to racism *within* the minority group. In common with many others on the left, the Australian author and journalist Jeff Sparrow has argued that anti-Muslim prejudice is now 'structurally identical' to the anti-Semitism of the 1930s.[32] This may be so, but anti-Semitism is also recrudescing in many parts of the world, and one reason for this is the increasing radicalisation of young Muslims by Islamic extremists. Of course, it ought to be possible to criticise anti-Semitism *and* anti-Muslim prejudice. And yet the indulgence often shown to certain conservative Muslims claiming to speak for their own communities leads many liberals to ignore the first thing for fear of seeming to engage in the second. Similarly, the anti-Semitism of black leaders such as Louis Farrakhan and Stokely Carmichael in the 1960s and 1970s often went unchallenged on the US left because to criticise it would have been to violate the cardinal rule of identity politics: if you're outside the group, you don't get to judge it.

This brings us to the final and most serious way in which identity politics can lead to racism, which has to do with the opportunity it presents for the far right and its fellow travellers. One of the weirder political phenomena of recent years has been the spectacle of the far right sticking up for Israel. And yet this weird phenomenon begins to look a little less strange when one considers that the right has decided to make the Islamic community its scapegoat du jour. Unable or unwilling to talk honestly about the tensions within the Islamic community, progressives have opened the door to a right that is only too happy to exaggerate the 'threat' from Muslim immigration, while casting itself as the champion and saviour of the white working class. In the United Kingdom, the filthy English Defence League revives memories of Oswald Mosley's Blackshirts, while the leader of the British National Party talks of 'Islamic colonisation'. Similarly, in the United States, a far-right organisation called Stop Islamization of America takes out ads on the New York City subway reading 'In any war between the civilized man and the savage, support the civilized man. Support Israel. Defeat Jihad.' Thus do the most repellent reactionaries rush in where progressives fear to tread.

In an article on Anders Behring Breivik, the far-right terrorist responsible for the murder of 77 Norwegians in 2011, the late Christopher Hitchens speculated on the 'symbiotic relationship' between the 'extreme jihadists' and 'their most virulent [far-right] opponents':

> In tapes and sermons from mosques in London and Hamburg, you may find whole manifestos about the need to keep women as chattel, to eradicate the disease of homosexuality, to thwart the Jewish design over international finance, and other fantasies of the Third Reich mentality. Pushed to its logical or pathological conclusion, this would involve something that Europeans and Americans have never seen before: a conflict between different forms of fascism in order to see which assault on multi-ethnic democracy was the most effective.[33]

Now more than ever a strong secular left is needed in order to resist these twin assaults. But it is only by distinguishing between 'multi-ethnic democracy' and the politics of identity and relativism — or, to put it another way, between multiculturalism as a description of reality and multiculturalism as an ideology — that the left can do so effectively. Sticking up for free speech and women's rights, even at the risk of offending those who claim to be offended already, is not imperialist, or even 'Western-centric'; it is simply what people on our side of politics *should do*. Again, Barbara Ehrenreich puts it beautifully: 'There can be no left where the only politics is a narrow politics of identity. We have to defend multiculturalism, but let's remember always that at its intellectual and moral core, the left isn't multi-anything.'[34]

CHAPTER FIVE

Don't Tread on Me

Self-pity has become central in the consciousness of the resurgent Right. Depicting themselves as victimised in any and every situation is not merely a fun game of upside down; it is essential to their self-understanding.

THOMAS FRANK, *PITY THE BILLIONAIRE*

'I'll tell you what, I have an idea!' hollered CNBC reporter Rick Santelli from the floor of the Chicago Board of Trade. 'You know, the new administration's big on computers and technology — how about this, President and new administration! Why don't you put up a website to have people vote on the internet as a referendum to see if we really want to subsidise the losers' mortgages? Or would we like to at least buy cars and buy houses in foreclosure and give them to people that might have a chance to actually prosper down the road, and reward people that could carry the water instead of drink the water?'[1]

The 'new administration' was new indeed; Santelli was speaking (or rather, shouting) on 19 February 2009, just 30 days after Barack Obama had been sworn in as President of the United States. Ordinarily, that would place him in what political commentators like to call 'the honeymoon period'; and yet Obama's plan, announced the previous day, to help nine million homeowners avoid foreclosure on their mortgages — just one in a suite of financial measures designed to sort out the economic mess bequeathed to him by his predecessor — had left Santelli feeling unromantic. Throwing out his arms like Joe Pesci in *Goodfellas*, and to whoops and whistles from the trading floor, he accused the new president of 'promoting bad behaviour'. In fact, he all but accused him of treason. Invoking at once the spectre of communism and the spirit of economic libertarianism, Santelli went into overdrive: 'This is America! How many of you people want to pay for your neighbour's mortgage that has an extra bathroom and can't pay their bills? Raise their [*sic*] hand.' The traders booed. 'President Obama, are you listening? ... You know, Cuba used to have mansions and a relatively decent economy. They moved from the individual to the collective and now they're driving '54 Chevys! ... We're thinking of having a Chicago tea party in July. All you capitalists that want to show up to Lake Michigan — I'm gonna start organising!'

Back in the studio, both presenters and panellists were amused by Santelli's outburst. Investor Wilbur Ross was smiling indulgently. 'Rick,' he joked, 'I congratulate you on your new incarnation as a revolutionary leader.' But Santelli was beyond irony — or else it was beyond him. 'Somebody needs one!' he bellowed into the camera, getting his pronouns spectacularly crossed. 'I'll tell you what, if you read our Founding Fathers, people like Benjamin Franklin and Jefferson, what we're doing in this country now is making them roll over in their graves.'

This caffeinated rant was patently ridiculous. Standing in front of the very constituency whose greed had brought the world economy low, Santelli labelled the President a communist for attempting to insulate the most vulnerable Americans against the ravages of the global financial crisis. And yet the reporter's words struck a resonant chord in the hearts of many middle-class Americans. His invocation of the Founding Fathers was just the ticket for a demographic in search of some overarching narrative in which to set its fear and disappointment. Wrapping himself in the Stars and Stripes, Santelli invited his viewers to believe that it wasn't America that had let them down but a few politicians that had let down America. America — the capital of capital — is pure. Left to its own devices, it will prosper. The losers lose, but only because they're losers. And the winners win, because they're winners. Only when politicians get involved do the losers win and the winners lose. And the upshot of *that* is that everyone loses.

It was the message the would-be winners wanted to hear, and Santelli's outburst soon went viral. Moreover, his idea of a 'tea party' protest quickly became a reality, and not just in Chicago but also across America. For the next three years, middle-class Americans would gather under placards reading 'Taxed enough already' (arranged vertically to form the acrostic 'TEA'), 'Party like it's 1773', 'Commander & thief', and 'Don't tread on me' (taken from the Gadsden flag, associated with the Continental Marines in the War of Independence). Some of them wore tri-corner hats; some had flutes and battle drums. All were possessed of the wrongheaded notion that the reasons for their misfortune had more to do with big government and its feckless beneficiaries than it did with the chaos of neoliberalism. Little wonder that the Chicago traders applauded Santelli to the very echo.

The Manufacturing of Dissent

Named for the famous protest against British taxation in 1773, the Tea Party movement was thus conceived in a moment of inspired cognitive dissonance. A lack of financial regulation had caused the global financial crisis, and now the government was attempting to cope with the consequences of that lack of regulation. By focusing on the second thing and not on the first, Santelli and his Tea Party followers managed to recast the GFC as the occasion for a power grab by the state rather than as a crisis of capitalism. Indeed, there *was* no crisis of capitalism, only a lack of faith in its beneficence. According to the Tea Party faithful, the proper response to the GFC was to push back against the power of government and reassert the primacy of the market. And so the ideas of Friedrich Hayek, Ludwig von Mises, and Milton Friedman — thinkers for whom any government interference was a step along the road to serfdom — began to enjoy renewed popularity at precisely the time when one might have expected them, and the policies they fathered, to fall into disfavour. 'Before 2009,' writes Thomas Frank in his superb book *Pity the Billionaire*, 'the man in the bread line did not ordinarily weep for the man lounging on his yacht.' But in the topsy-turvy world of the Tea Party movement, such 'reverse Marxism' was perfectly normal. It was, as Frank suggests, a bold 'switcheroo'.[2]

So audacious was this populist reversal that it needed a massive injection of emotion in order to achieve escape velocity. The tone was set by Santelli himself. His rant was an essay in indignation — so much so that many US commentators thought instantly of Howard Beale, the suicidal anchorman played by Peter Finch in the 1976 film *Network*. ('I'm as mad as hell and I'm not going to take it anymore!' screams Beale at the climax of his on-air tirades. This too would appear on Tea Party placards.) Nor was such ear-splitting indignation incidental to Tea Party ideology; on the contrary, it was central to it. Imaginary terrors need imaginary offences, and many were the populist *philosophes* on hand to help the Tea Party faithful surmount the cognitive barrier presented by the facts on the ground with calculated appeals to self-pity and resentment. 'From day one,' write Dick Armey and Matt Kibbe in *Give Us Liberty* (a 'Tea Party manifesto'), 'the good men and women who have risen up in peaceful dissent against a government that is bankrupting America have been subjected to the worst kinds of ridicule, name-calling, and downright hate.'[3] Thus a utopian and delusional ideology takes cover behind an unspoken imperative: *Be offended. Be very offended.*

From memory, it was the economist Paul Krugman, writing in *The New York Times*, who first used the term 'AstroTurf' in connection with the Tea Party. The implication was that this 'grassroots movement' was not really a grassroots movement at all, but the creation of established interests in the political and business sphere. Krugman had a point: though the majority of Tea Partiers seemed genuinely determined to resist the usual political suspects, many conservative politicians, think tanks, and media personalities rode the new wave of political dissent with more skill than Kelly Slater executing a late drop. Take Armey and Kibbe: given their line in folksy fellow-feeling, a reader could be forgiven for thinking that they'd never seen the inside of a country club. But in fact both men are *grands fromages* (chairman and president respectively) in an organisation called FreedomWorks, an influential conservative NPO with links back to the billionaire brothers David H. and Charles G. Koch. In thrall to the ideas of Hayek et al., the free-market 'activists' of FreedomWorks urge you to read such classics of economic libertarianism as Frédéric Bastiat's *The Law* (which they will send you a copy of, gratis!) and Ayn Rand's novel *Atlas Shrugged* (a gormless homage to *laissez-faire* capitalism, published in 1957). 'These, of course, are not new books,' write Armey and Kibbe in *Give Us Liberty*. 'Reading them, on the other hand, is a whole new generation of eyeballs.'[4]

On the Fox News channel, abominable showmen such as Glenn Beck gave voice (and direction) to Tea Party concerns, while on talkback radio, empurpled shock jocks managed to put political commentary on the same intellectual level as all-in wrestling. All played the offence card shamelessly. Talk-show host Michael Graham wrote a book with the indignant title *That's No Angry Mob, That's My Mom: Team Obama's assault on Tea-Party, talk-radio Americans* — a screed so unhinged that it actually manages to live up to its hysterical subtitle. In a weird development, some rightwing authors even affected to take offence *on behalf of the shock jocks taking offence* on behalf of the moms and dads of the Tea Party. In *Crimes Against Liberty: an indictment of President Barack Obama*, David Limbaugh goes in to bat for his persecuted brother Rush.[5] In this way, these seasoned media tough-guys set out to assure the Tea Party faithful that they didn't just sense their pain; they *shared* it.

In this enterprise, certain subjects proved invaluable. Take the use of the word 'teabagger' to describe a Tea Party sympathiser. Even allowing for American prudery, the feelings aroused by this appellation — one favoured by many liberals and leftwingers, and even employed by President Obama himself in an interview in 2009 — reveal a serious lack of proportion. Though the references to it are invariably coy (Limbaugh calls it 'a vulgar epithet involving a sexual act', and Armey and Kibbe a 'tasteless double entendre'),[6] this bit of locker-room humour occupies a central place in pro–Tea Party literature, and is always the occasion for a wail of self-pity. Or consider the (admittedly stupid) post on My.BarackObama.com, a re-election campaign website for President Obama, describing Tea Partiers as 'domestic terrorists'. Though the offending comments were deleted from the website, conservatives had a field day with them. Armey and Kibbe affected to regard them as part of an 'offensive narrative',[7] while Graham could scarcely contain himself: '[A]s a talk radio host and writer, I get called names all the time. No complaints — it comes with the job. I'm used to it. But these comments weren't just aimed at me. As a bona fide Tea Partier, my mom was also a target.'[8]

All of this must have worked to some degree, because what Frank calls 'the political economy of self-pity' soon began to overwhelm the movement to which Graham and others had attached themselves. In fact, Frank suggests that a 'second-remove grievance' came to overshadow the original cause: 'Now people protested not only to advertise their views on a given issue but *out of resentment at the insults heaped upon the protesters*.'[9] Once a bloodcurdling threat to the British, the Gadsden flag's slogan, 'Don't tread on me', was fast becoming the ensign of hurt feelings.

I'm with Stupid

The sense of victimhood is so central to the Tea Party, and to the contemporary populist right in general, that it is difficult to overestimate. But of what, or whom, are the victims victims? In the past, the populist right would select some 'out group' or minority to act as the scapegoat for society's ills and the obstacle to its rejuvenation; communists, Freemasons, Catholics, and Jews have all taken their turn in the stocks. Yet today, conservative paranoia has alighted not on an out group but on an in group. It has alighted on the state itself.

Of course, there are many excellent reasons to adopt a sceptical attitude towards the state. But the populist right's contempt for government is morbid and obsessional. Read any of the Tea Party's conservative screeds, or peruse the placards at a Tea Party rally, and the want of proportion and reason will be obvious. Underlying all of them is a notion of society as irrevocably split between the people and the elites. These are not economic but political elites — *liberal* political elites, to be precise, for liberals gravitate to Washington, DC as surely as geese fly south for the winter. It is a fundamental principle of this vision that having a lot of money in the bank does not preclude a claim to ordinariness; as Frank notes, even big-city traders get to 'wear the halo of common-man averageness' in the right's economic libertarian fantasy. (When Santelli delivered his rant to camera, he referred to the traders surrounding him — the ones making zoo noises — as 'the silent majority'.) In this way, the right can command popular sympathy and stoke popular indignation while advocating policies, such as low taxation and deregulation, that lead directly to economic inequality. For them, the market is the real election, and the elected representative merely an impostor.

Sophisticated liberals — the eggheads and know-it-alls who've never done a proper day's work in their lives — excite a special animus. There is a rich vein of anti-intellectualism running through US conservatism, and commentators such as Graham and Limbaugh are never happier than when waxing hysterical about the left's intellectual arrogance. Here is Graham in full flow:

> [T]he politicians who govern us right now have almost nothing in common with their people. All of those kooky ideas you used to snicker at in college, all those campus nuts who wouldn't shut up about how smart they were, but who knew nothing about the real world — they're the ones in charge.
>
> The challenge is for typical Americans like my mom to 'cling' desperately to our fundamental values of personal responsibility, economic opportunity, and common sense. These used to be the shared ideals among nearly all Americans. But in Obama's America, they're considered symptoms of political dementia.
>
> There's nothing wrong with you, Mom. They're wrong, and you're right. So right, in fact, that instead of answering your concerns about bailouts, stimulus spending, and healthcare, they just attack you.[10]

This may be self-satirising, but its blend of chippiness and lachrymosity, its bracingly unsophisticated nod to 'the real world' and to 'common sense', and its clumsy attempt to transform Mrs G into an everyman — or everymom — is a good illustration of the demagoguery currently employed on the populist right. Affecting to speak truth to power, and to deplore the arrogance of the liberal elite, Graham and his fellow blowhards at once whip up and weaponise offence.

President Obama is, of course, a gift to the anti-intellectual movement. Eloquent and intelligent — in stark contrast to his predecessor — Obama is exactly the kind of politician on whom conservative populists love to train their guns. Misinterpreting his self-assurance for priggishness, they refer habitually to his contemptuousness, his air of superiority, his thin-skinned arrogance.[11] According to Graham, 'there has never been a president who had as little in common with the citizens he governs as Barack Obama' — an absurd claim, even by his own high standards.[12] At its worst, this sort of schtick is apt to descend into a kind of rhetorical ignorance whereby any word of more than two syllables is seen as evidence of contempt for the masses, whose (assumed) confusion is in turn adduced as evidence of their folksy wisdom. Having decided, reasonably enough, that being intelligent doesn't make you right about everything, many populist commentators behave as if the opposite holds true.

If demagoguery were diving, this plonking non sequitur would be a double somersault with twist and pike, but such 'thinking' has undoubtedly influenced events. How else to explain the ludicrous choice of Sarah Palin as John McCain's running mate for the 2008 presidential election if not by reference to the dialectic in which scepticism about intellectuals morphs into adulation of the dumb? The problem for the left, or at least for the US Democrats, was that any aspersions about Palin's intelligence tended to confirm the suspicions of her supporters regarding those on the other side of the aisle. Thus, the self-styled Mama Grizzly, whose slogan was 'Don't retreat — reload!', became the focus of vicarious self-pity. In *The Persecution of Sarah Palin*, Matthew Continetti scrapes together and carefully itemises every smear and unsubstantiated bit of gossip to have issued from the lips of arrogant liberals regarding the former mayor of Wasilla. According to him, 'The reaction to Sarah Palin was visceral, nasty, and unrelenting.'[13] Needless to say, it would be possible — in fact, laughably easy — to compile a comparable dossier on the 'visceral, nasty, and unrelenting' reaction to Barack Obama's presidency. But the point is not the accuracy or otherwise of Continetti's claims, nor any want of balance on his part; the point is that he regards offence as a sure-fire way to motivate the base.

Bonfire of the Inanities

There is an odd sense of unreality about the way in which, as Frank puts it, 'these hymners of Darwinian struggle, of the freedom to fail, of competition to the death, advance their war on the world by means of tearful weepy-woo.'[14] In a way, one has to admire such brazenness, if brazenness is what it is; after all, it takes a lot of front to appear so spectacularly affronted all the time, especially when your side still holds all the cards. And yet we shouldn't admire it too much, for running beneath this river of tears are some very nasty currents indeed.

One current is discernible in a popular work of American literature. In *The Bonfire of the Vanities* — published in 1987, the year in which Allan Bloom published *The Closing of the American Mind* — Tom Wolfe paints a picture of New York City as caught up in an intense and vertiginous swirl of political opportunism, cynicism, demagoguery, and hucksterism of every kind. Wolfe's protagonist is Sherman McCoy, a Wall Street bond dealer (or 'Master of the Universe') going broke on roughly one million dollars a year. Involved in a hit-and-run incident that leaves a young black man in hospital, McCoy becomes a lightning rod for a cynical and sensationalist press, and a convenient scapegoat for two interests: Abe Weiss, the Jewish district attorney angling for re-election and stung by accusations from the black community that there is one law for whites and another for blacks; and the black community itself, whose 'leaders' (especially Reverend Bacon, a preacher and civil-rights activist modelled on Jesse Jackson and Al Sharpton) choose to regard the hit-and-run as an instance of, and metaphor for, the racism of US society in general. At the novel's climax, both these interests are disappointed when the presiding judge, Myron Kovitsky, dismisses the charges against McCoy. The anti-McCoy protesters outside the courtroom erupt in fury:

> *That's Kovitsky! That's the one!* Shouts … a tremendous rumble … BRRAAAANNNGGG! — the alarm battered and battered and ricocheted off the marble, doubling, trebling … An older man, not a demonstrator, came up from the side, as if to confront Kovitsky, pointing and shouting, 'You …' Sherman lunged at him and screamed: 'Get your fucking face outta the way!' The man jumped back, his mouth open. His *expression* — frightened! *Now!* — *again!* — drive a fist into his belly, mash his nose into a pulp, ram a heel into his eye! — Sherman turned to look at Kovitsky.
>
> Kovitsky was staring at him the way you'd stare at a lunatic.[15]

Kovitsky may regard McCoy as a lunatic, but it is clear that Wolfe regards him as a hero, or at least as an incipient one. For most of the novel, this pampered WASP has been at the mercy of Jews and African Americans. But in the book's final paragraphs he begins to fight back, and planted in this fight-back is the seed of self-respect. And not only self-respect for McCoy, but also for white middle-class Protestant Americans in general. For why, asks Wolfe, should pride in one's identity be the preserve of ethnic communities only? If you can't beat them, join them; that is Wolfe's 'message', a message that anyone who'd read his journalism — his mocking, unforgiving portraits of credulous liberals in thrall to the Black Panthers, or of 'shit-eating' white bureaucrats being taken for a ride by black gangsters in the slums of San Francisco — would not have been surprised to hear.[16] Contemptuous of the so-called novel of ideas, Wolfe would no doubt reject the notion that his art has a palpable design on us. And yet somewhere in the bonfire of his imagination the phoenix of white dignity spreads its wings.

The date, 1987, is significant. For it was around that time that New York became a 'majority-minority city': a city in which non-Hispanic whites accounted for less than 50 per cent of the population. *The Bonfire of the Vanities* gave vent to the anxieties attendant on that demographic change, while also pointing an accusing finger at the inverted racism and brazen demagoguery of black community leaders especially. But as well as capturing the spirit of its time, the novel in some ways anticipates our own. (Remember that Rick Santelli's cheerleaders were Masters of the Universe, too.) For, 25 years after it first hit the shelves, the change that overcame New York is about to overcome the United States as a whole. And it is, surely, partly for this reason that when we cup an ear towards the populist right we can discern — albeit only faintly — the stirrings of a white identity politics.

These stirrings are rarely explicit, and may even be for the most part unconscious. Certainly, former president Jimmy Carter went far too far when he told *NBC News* that he thought the 'overwhelming proportion of the intensely demonstrated animosity toward President Barack Obama is based on the fact that he is a black man, he's African American'.[17] Similarly, the comedian Janeane Garofalo's characterisation of the Tea Party movement as barely distinguishable from the Ku Klux Klan ('This is racism, straight up. That is nothing but a bunch of teabagging rednecks') was nasty and inaccurate.[18] But the fact remains that this largely white movement, focusing on fiscal and constitutional issues, often betrays a note of racial resentment strongly reminiscent of the kind of rhetoric that met the rise of political correctness.

That rhetoric is perhaps best characterised as a species of political jujitsu, whereby the opposition's strengths are used against it. Or, to escalate the metaphor, it is as if the right had picked up the grenade that had fallen with a muddy splat in its own trench and lobbed it back in the direction of the enemy. For it is clear that many Tea Partiers see themselves as on the losing side in a war in which the formerly persecuted have themselves become the persecutors. In *The Tea Party and the Remaking of Republican Conservatism*, Theda Skocpol and Vanessa Williamson present polling data which shows that Tea Party supporters 'are even more likely than other conservatives to believe that racial minorities are held back by their own personal failings'.[19] And while such views are rarely articulated, the imagery of the movement can sometimes seem like a standing challenge to the whole idea that society's poorest elements have anyone but themselves to blame.

Take the massive rally organised by Fox News presenter Glenn Beck in the US fall of 2010. Entitled 'Restoring Honor' and billed as a celebration of America's 'heroes and heritage', this event drew a large Tea Party contingent and was seen by many as an attempt by Beck, a media buffoon and shameless self-promoter with the seeming ability to cry at will, to put his stamp on the swell of populist sentiment that began in early 2009. But the really interesting thing about the rally was the fact that it was held at the location (the Lincoln Memorial in Washington, DC) and on the anniversary (28 August) of Martin Luther King's 'I Have a Dream' speech. Of course, Beck denied any intended parallel; indeed, he denied that the Restoring Honor rally had any political content at all, choosing instead to package it as a cross between an evangelical sermon and a fundraiser for war veterans. Yet the event told a different story. In her speech on the day, Sarah Palin compared the rally's participants to the civil-rights activists of the 1960s, while Beck let it be known that he'd spent the night in the very hotel in which Dr King had polished his homily.[20] To a casual observer such as me, the 'I Have a Dream' comparison seemed as blatant as it could be without being explicit, which just leaves the question of why the organisers thought the comparison meaningful at all.

The implication seemed, at least to me, to be that a new form of discrimination — one as egregious as the official racism against which King had set his face — was at large in the modern United States. Yes, the populists' real target was the overweening, overstuffed state; but with an African American at the head of that state, new opportunities for rabble-rousing had arisen. For the dog-whistling demagogue eager to appeal to the unconscious fears of white Americans, what could be more efficacious than a suggestion (or an insinuation) that it was on *your* shoulders that the mantle of victim now rested? In the summer of 2009, Beck had run into trouble for saying that Obama had a 'deep-seated hatred for white people'.[21] Could it be that the rally at the Lincoln Memorial spoke to some vague and unarticulated anxiety that white America had ceased to be prepotent? It is hard to make such a generalisation, but the near-absence of black faces in the crowd was hardly an encouraging sign, while the monotonous regularity with which the charge of racism was denied from the podium served, as Christopher Hitchens noted, only to raise suspicions further.[22] I'm not alleging any sort of conscious racism. But between the placard reading 'It doesn't matter what this sign says; you'll call it racist anyway' and the T-shirt labelling Barack Obama a 'socialist, a fraud, a liar and a racist bigot' — between sensitivity to the charge, and indulgence in the accusation, of racism — there exists a welter of ill-defined feelings — anxieties, disappointments, resentments, and frustrations — that some demagogues of the populist right may be only too happy to exploit for their own purposes.

Political Jujitsu

Take the right's demagogue-in-chief, Rush Limbaugh, a man so comfortable playing the reverse-racism card one is forced to wonder if he's using a full deck. Here he is on his eponymous radio show on 15 September 2009, sounding off about a CCTV video in which a group of black children attack a white schoolmate:

> It's Obama's America, is it not? Obama's America, white kids [are] getting beaten up on school buses now. You put your kids on a school bus, you expect safety but in Obama's America the white kids now get beat up with the black kids cheering, 'Yay, right on, right on, right on, right on,' and, of course, everybody says the white kid deserved it, he was born a racist, he's white.[23]

My argument in this book is that a person should always be able to explain *why* he or she is offended — that argument and articulation are nearly always better than raw emotion. But contemplating this ridiculous tirade, I admit to a sense of exhaustion. For where do we start with this quote? With the notion that kids could walk the streets or ride the buses in safety before a black man sauntered through the doors of the White House? With the idea that schoolchildren were suddenly emboldened by Obama's election in 2008? With the fact that nothing in the video suggests any racial animus on the part of the attackers? With that vicious bit of minstrelsy ('Yay, right on, right on …')? With that paranoid pronoun, 'everybody'? With the nastiness and cynicism in the statement?

Let's start with the bus, for buses have played a crucial cameo in the populist conservative renaissance. Conservative blowhards particularly love to allude to the segregated bus — that symbol of racial discrimination. For example, here is Limbaugh again, responding to the appointment of Sonia Sotomayor to the Supreme Court in May 2009, and to the revelation that Sotomayor had once given a speech in which she'd suggested that in issues of sex and race discrimination, it might be better to defer to those who'd been on the receiving end of both:

> How do you get promoted in a Barack Obama administration? By hating white people. Or even saying you do … make white people a new oppressed minority … *They're moving to the back of the bus* [my italics] … That's the modern day Republican Party. The equivalent of the old South. The new oppressed minority.[24]

Notwithstanding his impressionistic grammar, the man once described as 'the titular head of the Republican Party' could not be clearer: white Americans are the new black Americans, and racial 'sensitivity' the new racial prejudice. Segregation is back, but in negative. Little wonder that a grainy video of a white student getting attacked on a bus should have inspired such a livid, vivid tableau.

Nor is Limbaugh the only commentator to invoke the

shade of segregation with reference to the public transit system. When Barack Obama compared the US economy to a car that had been driven into a ditch by the previous administration, suggesting that the Republicans were now banished to the back seats, some Fox talking heads chose to interpret it as a veiled reference to segregation, implying that Obama was settling old scores — getting his own back on white America for the indignities it had visited upon African Americans. Fox News legal analyst Peter Johnson Jr was one such. 'It's a peculiar and strange and haunting and really backward reference that we're seeing by the President,' he opined, continuing:

> What we're really seeing is a reference to the notion of being in the back of the bus. That's a matter of sad American history, embarrassing American history ... So now we have a president referring to this kind of malignant, charged era in American history and saying in a long narrative, and it's incredible what he said, that somehow the car's in a ditch ... And once the car is out of the ditch and the Republicans demand the keys — you can't have the keys, but we'll let you sit in the back of the bus.[25]

Johnson's elaborate deconstruction of the President's remarks continued a venerable Fox tradition whereby you make your own news in the process of reporting it. A far more impressive bit of textual analysis came courtesy of *The Daily Show*'s Jon Stewart. 'If this is a racial metaphor,' said

Stewart, addressing himself to Johnson and others, 'you aren't Rosa Parks; you're Miss Daisy.'[26]

Such conservative tactics are easy to mock. But it seems that US politicians are also increasingly willing to stoop to them. In March 2012, Newt Gingrich took ostentatious offence at a quip by the actor Robert De Niro. De Niro, who was introducing First Lady Michelle Obama at a fundraising dinner, asked the audience whether it thought the United States was ready for a 'white First Lady' — a reference to the upcoming general election, for which Gingrich was among those seeking the Republican nomination. ('No!' shouted one diner, to which the actor replied, 'Too soon, right?') Needless to say, this neat inversion, far from being an instance of racial discrimination, was in fact a joke at its expense. And yet Gingrich affected to treat the gag as evidence of racial bigotry. 'I do want to say one thing on behalf of both [*sic*] my wife, and on behalf of Karen Santorum, and on behalf of Ann Romney,' said Gingrich, referring to the women whose Republican husbands each hoped to face off against Obama in November, 'and that is I think Robert De Niro is wrong … I think the country is ready for a new First Lady, and he doesn't have to describe it in racial terms … I call on the President to apologise for him.'[27] (Happily, the President didn't apologise, though the First Lady's press secretary Olivia Alair did concede that the joke was 'inappropriate'.) Or consider the spectacle of Mitt Romney — the man who ended up filling the shoes so coveted by the thin-skinned Gingrich — taking offence at an innocuous comment by the 'gaffe-prone' vice president, Joe Biden, towards the end of the 2012 presidential election. Biden had suggested that Romney's plan to 'unchain' Wall Street if he won the presidency would end up putting 'y'all *in* chains' — a decent enough summation, in my view, of the way in which 'economic freedom' tends to entrain its opposite. But the Republican nominee saw an opportunity to stoke offence, and seized the poker with both manicured hands. Hadn't Biden insinuated that Romney proposed to bring back slavery, or at least that he was unsympathetic to the historical plight of African Americans? George W. Bush's former speechwriter, Matt Latimer, was also beside himself with indignation. 'Does Joe Biden, an attorney with an ego as big as his mouth, actually believe a president could reinstate slavery if he wanted to?'[28] Clearly, Biden had not indicated he believed anything of the kind. But the charge of offence is now so compelling that it has ceased to need any grounding in reality in order to work its political magic.

Like all magic, this political magic involves much chicanery and smoke, much sleight-of-hand and misdirection. But while magic depends on the audience's willingness to be deceived, the conjurers of offence and sensitivity tap into something far more primal: into fear and frustration and blamefulness and hate. This is the essence of demagoguery, and its effect is to create a citizenry that is less engaged than *enraged* — angry without being intellectually active. It isn't what you think that counts, says the populist mountebank, but how you feel. And according to him, you should feel offended.

CHAPTER SIX

————

I Feel, Therefore I Am

As a narcissistic personality type, the ruling personality type of our day, I take considerable pride in my inner world. The alienating environments in which I regularly find myself feel like an implicit diss of my self-importance. Everyone is just passing me by, like I pass them by, as if I were just another body crowding the sidewalk, the highway, or the corridors of cyberspace. These other bodies crowding the space I am trying to navigate seem ignorant and oblivious to the greatness of my inner world. And so I compensate for all the thousand-thousand abrasions and irritations to my self-importance by inflating my inner world. I take excessive and brittle pride in my inner world as the best, most valid, most real, most everything inner world to be found anywhere.

JONATHAN ZAP, 'TRANSCENDING ONLINE ROAD RAGE'

If only Yumi Stynes, a co-host of Network Ten's morning gabfest *The Circle* (an unsightly boil, now thankfully lanced, on the arse of Australian daytime television), had consulted Rudyard Kipling before leaving for work on 28 February 2012, she might have saved herself a whole heap of trouble. Certainly a glance at the rollicking 'Tommy' would not have done her any harm, given that it inveighs against witless sniggering at people prepared to die for their country. But Kipling's couplet, 'makin' mock o' uniforms that guard you while you sleep / Is cheaper than them uniforms, an' they're starvation cheap', had, on this particular day, clearly slipped the presenter's mind. Consequently, in response to some poolside footage of Corporal Ben Roberts-Smith — a highly decorated and lavishly tattooed Aussie warrior — exercising his Hulk-like physique, Yumi Stynes commented: 'He's going to dive down to the bottom of the pool to see if his brain is there.'[1]

Now, everyone knows that people who spend their lives in the gym aren't always the sharpest tools in the shed, if for no other reason than that time spent on the Thighmaster is time spent *not* reading Thucydides. And it's also true that Roberts-Smith's torso called to mind Clive James's description of the actor Arnold Schwarzenegger as 'a brown condom full of walnuts'.[2] But as a soldier who had recently received the Victoria Cross after single-handedly attacking two machine-gun emplacements while on his third tour in Afghanistan, Roberts-Smith could perhaps be forgiven for wanting to keep in peak condition. Certainly the man who already sported the Medal for Gallantry on his mighty left pec didn't deserve to have his brains brought into question by someone who'd clearly left hers in the car.

In short, it was an idiotic comment, amplified by the ersatz levity with which it was greeted in the Ten studio, and by speculation from Stynes's co-host, George Negus, about a possible disjunct between a man's physical attributes and his sexual prowess. ('I'm sure he's a really good guy, nothing about poor old Ben. But that sort of bloke — what if they're not up to it in the sack?')[3] But an idiotic comment is all it was — a vacuous remark by a person under pressure to fill the intellectual vacuum that is commercial daytime television. I'm as sure as I can be that no treasonous intent was operating in Stynes's breast when she made it, no desire to poison the Australian polity or give encouragement to its enemies. And yet the campaign of abuse with which it was met came as close as language can to a lynching.

'Shame shame shame you idiots its [*sic*] disgusting' ... 'I can't believe they would speak so trashy [*sic*] about a guy who would do anything for our country' ... 'My neighbour is a ww2 vetran [*sic*] at kokoda you have tarnished the whole aussie defence force, IDIOTS' ... 'So ashamed by the hosts of @thecircle, esp Yumi, they should be taken off TV, its trashy rubbish anyway... Ben Roberts-Smith is a hero #shame' ... 'He's the epitome of a great Aussie bloke! What a disgusting comment by this bird brain "Yumi". Who is she?'

Those were some of the milder comments to appear on Twitter and *The Circle*'s Facebook page. Others called for Stynes to apologise, which she did, and for her to be sacked, which she wasn't, though the ostentatious exodus of sponsors from the program perhaps precipitated its cancellation a few months later. Still others declared the half-Japanese Stynes to be an 'ugly slut' and a 'half-caste bitch' and made physical threats against her two young children. (Stynes's on-air apology was reported in Melbourne's *Herald Sun* under the headline 'Yumi So Sorry' — a seemingly nasty bit of ventriloquism in the register once known as 'yellow face'.) The more the story was covered in the press, the bigger and more ridiculous it became. It was a screaming match and a free-for-all. Never, it seemed, had daytime television so lived up to Ian McEwan's description of it as the 'democrat's pornography'.[4]

Then again, this orgy of recrimination, while unusual in its intensity, was hardly an uncommon occurrence. Looking through my notes for this chapter, I find hundreds of examples of similar 'controversies' — some about barely anything at all. For example, on a single day in May 2011, I happened upon four 'offence' stories: one involving *Sesame Street*, to which various US conservatives had objected on account of its 'liberal agenda'; one involving Naomi Campbell, the Afro-British supermodel, whose appearance in an ad for a chocolate bar had sparked allegations of racism; one involving Lewis Hamilton, the racing driver (also Afro-British), whose lighthearted comment to the Formula One press pack regarding his frequent run-ins with the stewards — 'Maybe it's because I'm black. That's what Ali G says!' — had itself occasioned a run-in with the stewards; and one involving MTV's 'reality' jerkfest *Geordie Shore*, which many residents of Newcastle-Upon-Tyne, the city in the north of England from which the show's participants were drawn, regarded as a defamation. Mass entertainment will always divide the viewing public; no culture is monolithic, and what one 'demographic' finds fresh and irreverent another will regard as pornographic and heretical. But in the early years of the 21st century, offence has *itself* become a form of entertainment — a source of morbid, masochistic pleasure, bittersweet as a Campari cocktail. How else to explain such monsters of rudeness as US radio thug Rush Limbaugh, or his Australian doppelganger Alan Jones, a man so full of bile and spite that he would intrude upon a prime minister's grief with the observation that her recently deceased father had died of 'shame' because of her lies?[5] Thus, those whose *raison d'être* is to take offence on behalf of their constituencies grant themselves leave to dole it out, and the whole unsightly business quickly becomes self-generating.

In our eagerness to take offence, we make ourselves a prey to the demagogue. Politicians know what plays, and are only too happy to play on our feelings: to chip in with a solemn condemnation or a bit of ostentatious head-shaking when doing so will bring a dash of populist pizzazz to the grey, Sisyphean business of politics. And so it comes as no surprise to find the Australian defence minister Stephen Smith describing Stynes's comment as 'reprehensible' (even as the unfortunate woman was being so roundly reprehended as to cause her employers to fear for her safety), or to find Kevin Rudd, as prime minister of

Australia, attempting to give himself a lift in the polls by describing the work of a lauded photographer as 'absolutely revolting' because it depicted naked pubescent bodies. Never mind that Bill Henson's studies of the human form are tender and touching and so far from exploitative as to recall to mind the anxiety and awkwardness of adolescence; once the Sydney constabulary, acting on a handful of complaints, had removed a number of his pictures from view, and the talkback blowhards had begun to have their fun, Rudd saw his cue and spoke his lines perfectly. His 'opinion' — of which he availed himself, appropriately enough, on daytime television — was a clear attempt to buy popular sentiment at the expense of an artist's autonomy. 'Shame shame shame' indeed.

Really Neat People

How did we arrive in this age of rage, this curious disstopia? The answer to that question is complicated and will involve much speculation, but I am convinced that it has to do with the increasing personalisation of politics. By this I don't mean the cult of the strong leader or the indebtedness of modern pollies to the dark arts of image-making and spin, but rather the way in which we, the public, experience politics in the 21st century — not as necessary civic engagement but as a clash of identities, as an expression of (or assault upon) our individuality. And by 'politics' I mean not only our views on tax or liberal intervention, but also the attitude we choose to adopt when a ditzy purveyor of 'infotainment' makes a dull-witted comment about an Australian war hero. For politics isn't only what happens in parliament, or at the party meeting or the union demo. Politics is what happens between our ears. And that we now have the tools and the inclination to make what happens between our ears available to everyone is in some ways the cause, and in some ways the effect, of the culture of offence and sensitivity.

This degeneration runs beneath and around and into the assorted ideologies and demagogueries dealt with in this book: the controversies over political correctness, multiculturalism, and identity politics, and the wave of populist indignation currently engulfing US politics. It is a degeneration most poetically characterised by the title of Todd Gitlin's splendid book, *The Twilight of Common Dreams*, except that the twilight has since become night, and the dreams transmogrified into feverish nightmares. The ubiquity of offence is one indication of a huge eruption in the common soil; the commingling of political and personal concerns that has taken place over the last half century has combined with modern information technology to engender a new identity politics, or politics of identification. The result is not politics in the traditional sense, nor political indifference, but something in between — a heady brew of narcissism and allegiance, the outward manifestations of which are the moan of self-pity and the snarl of resentment, the indignant grab and the abusive post.

The phrase 'the personal is political' comes from an article by Carol Hanisch published in 1970 in *Notes from the Second Year: women's liberation*. Hanisch's article is a spirited defence of 'consciousness-raising', by which members of the Women's Liberation Movement would share their experiences of male oppression in an effort to personalise the struggle for liberation, to emphasise how inequality and prejudice operate at the level of lived experience. For many feminists, this approach smacked of therapy — of self-indulgent navel-gazing — but for Hanisch and her fellow activists in the New York Radical Women group, the method was an important weapon in the battle against unequal treatment. In fact, Hanisch did not entirely disavow the label of 'therapy' when it came to consciousness-raising, though her preference was for 'political therapy' rather than merely 'personal therapy'. 'The most important thing is getting rid of self-blame,' she wrote. 'Can you imagine what would happen if women, blacks, and workers ... would stop blaming ourselves for our sad situations? It seems to me the whole country needs that kind of political therapy ... What [the consciousness-raiser] says basically is that women are really neat people.'[6]

The idea that the personal is political, which became synonymous with second-wave feminism, did not develop in a cultural vacuum. Since at least the early 1960s a notion had been gathering force: that traditional politics had failed to take account of 'the emotional deficit' in modern life. This sense of estrangement and alienation, of disillusion with formal politics, is apparent in the Port Huron Statement, the manifesto of the US organisation Students for a Democratic Society (SDS) and the de facto founding document of the agglomeration of movements that marched under the ensign of the New Left. Completed in 1962, and written substantially by the SDS's Tom Hayden, the statement called for a 'participatory democracy' based on non-violent civil disobedience; and although it cited many concerns with which more traditional liberals and leftists would have been in sympathy (such as the struggle for civil rights), it was also an expression of youthful angst against the prevailing adult order, steeped in the cloying language of self: 'Men have unrealised potential for self-cultivation, self-direction, self-understanding, and creativity … The goal of man and society should be human independence: a concern not with image of popularity [*sic*] but with finding a meaning in life that is personally authentic.' Getting his retaliation in first, Hayden sought to defend his doctrine against the charge of 'egoistic individualism': 'The object is not to have one's way so much as it is to have a way of one's own.'[7] No doubt there were plenty of cultural warriors on the other side of the ideological aisle who regarded that as a distinction without a difference.

If so, that would not be entirely fair. Of course it is the case that radical politics would be as hollow as a bongo drum unless it effected, or proposed to effect, some fundamental change in an individual's sense of being. It is more than flirting with tautology to say that the whole point of being a radical is to change the relations of society with a view to changing the people within it — to give them greater control over their destinies, to enable them to be *happier*. In this sense, the personal *is* political, and has been since time immemorial. And yet, when the discourses of personal development and political liberation fuse too seamlessly — when the one register borrows too liberally from the other — it is often a sign that personal ends are being mistaken for political ones. From there, it is only a hop and a skip to a view of politics as an *expression* of the personal — from a situation, in other words, in which the personal begins to define the political. Beginning from the proposition that the personal is political, we end up behaving as if the converse is true, that the political is personal.

This inversion is neatly encapsulated in a passage from David Lodge's novel of campus shenanigans *Changing Places*, published in 1975 but set in 1969, on the eve of what Tom Wolfe described, in one of his better moments, as the 'Me Decade'. Philip Swallow, a British lecturer teaching at a US university, is walking through the campus in the aftermath of a political vigil of the kind favoured by Tom Hayden and his chums on the New Left:

> He strolled across Howle Plaza, soaking up the sunshine, past the booths and stalls of student political groups — a kind of ideological fair, this, at which you could join SDS, buy the literature of the Black Panthers, contribute to the

Garden Bail Fund, pledge yourself to Save the Bay, give blood to the Viet Cong, obtain leaflets on first-aid in gas attacks, sign a petition to legalise pot, and express yourself in a hundred other interesting ways.[8]

It was John Stuart Mill, in *On Liberty*, who first used the metaphor of the marketplace of ideas to suggest the way in which 'free competition' between differing viewpoints serves to safeguard the truth. But in the above passage Lodge moves the metaphor on to imply the commodification of ideas. His vision of an 'ideological fair' at which the student activist seeks opportunities to 'express [him]self' is really an allegation of the activist's complicity in the very culture of shallow individualism against which he sets his face. So the causes to which young radicals might be expected to commit themselves, pooling a little of their individuality in the process, are regarded instead as the occasion for a noisy affirmation of that individuality — a step along the road to self-expression, which is to say the only cause that counts.

The Triumph of Self-esteem

It was not until the 1970s that the culture of self-expression (and self-absorption) really began to dominate, and not until the end of that decade that this culture found its greatest critic in the historian and moralist Christopher Lasch. In his peerless study *The Culture of Narcissism*, published in 1979, Lasch suggested that the 1970s were characterised by a shallow individualism, 'a narcissistic preoccupation with the self'. 'After the political turmoil of the sixties,' he wrote,

> Americans have retreated to purely personal preoccupations. Having no hope of improving their lives in any of the ways that matter, people have convinced themselves that what matters is psychic self-improvement: getting in touch with their feelings, eating health food, taking lessons in ballet or belly-dancing, immersing themselves in the wisdom of the East, jogging, learning how to 'relate', overcoming the 'fear of pleasure'. Harmless in themselves, these pursuits, elevated to a program and wrapped in the rhetoric of authenticity and awareness, signify a retreat from politics and a repudiation of the recent past.[9]

That last point is especially important, for it was through its rejection of the past and its concomitant fetishisation of the new that the counterculture softened itself up to the very forces it claimed to reject — the dialectic that Lodge identified as at work in his ideological fair. As Lasch put it: 'Strategies of narcissistic survival now present themselves as emancipation from the repressive conditions of the past, thus giving rise to a "cultural revolution" that reproduces the worst features of the collapsing civilisation it claims to criticise.'

Again, trends in the 1960s anticipated this development. In his study of that decade, *The Neophiliacs*, Christopher

Booker identified newness and the love of the new ('neophilia') as one of its defining traits.[10] But, again, it was in the 1970s that this obsession with newness, and with *now*ness, really began to dominate. 'To live for the moment is the prevailing passion,' wrote Lasch, before arguing that when people cease to regard themselves as part of a continuum they not only lose their sense of the future (and so of political possibility) but also fall prey to the temporary satisfactions, the ephemeral consolations, of the market:

> In a simpler time, advertising merely called attention to the product and extolled its advantages. Now it manufactures a product of its own: the consumer, perpetually unsatisfied, restless, anxious, and bored. Advertising serves not so much to advertise products as to promote consumption as a way of life.[11]

Thus, the 1960s counterculture became the 'alternative' culture of the 1970s, a riot of diverse enthusiasms in which the market economy was only too happy to play the role of provocateur. In short, whatever the alternative culture was an alternative *to*, it wasn't capitalism.

In the 1970s, Westerners learned to love themselves, to grant themselves permission to be happy, or angry, or horny, or silly, or whatever. And attendant on this self-regard was an ostentatious sense of introspection — what the sociologist and social commentator Frank Furedi calls 'therapy culture': the prevalence of emotionalism in politics

and culture, of self-disclosure or emotional 'sharing', of
the dread assumption that personal tribulations must have
an impersonal resonance. Like Lasch, Furedi sees this
phenomenon as related to the collapse of the left: the old
left looked forward to a society in which justice would be
available to all; but upon waking from that noble dream,
the left internalised and individualised the emphasis on
human potential. Turning its back on the ecstatic notion
that human beings could change the world, the New Left
began to focus instead on helping people to survive their
circumstances.

It should be obvious that we in the early 21st century
are the heirs to this culture of narcissism. The hysterical
self-exposure of daytime television, misery memoirs, and
the tearful interview — these are the symptoms of therapy
culture, witnesses to the triumph of self-esteem, to the idea
that you are what you *feel* about yourself. In the late 1990s
I worked in a bookshop in a bohemian patch of North
West London and watched the self-help section expand to
the point where we had to dispense with the back office
to accommodate the tsunami of new titles. These books —
which ranged from studies in astrology, to 'conversations'
with this or that deity, to paeans to the latest miracle
fungus — were as self-important as their covers were
gaudy; even George Eliot's Casaubon, with his 'Key to All
Mythologies', would be loath to display such intellectual
hubris as the grinning guru with the headset microphone.
Our best and most consistent seller was *The Prophet* by

Kahlil Gibran, the Lebanese-American artist and writer whose windy mystical generalities seemed to me and my fellow booksellers (sulking over our takeaway coffees in the shop's new, subterranean staffroom) to encapsulate the spirit of the times. 'Spare me the political events and power struggles,' Gibran implored, 'as the whole Earth is my homeland and all men are my fellow countrymen.'[12] Or as the US president puts it in the 1996 film *Mars Attacks!*, shortly before he is slaughtered by aliens, 'Why can't we all just ... *get along?*'

The New Self-esteem

It's probably inadvisable, when attempting to sketch the hollowing-out of selfhood in advanced capitalist society, to employ formulations of the 'new black' variety. (You know the kind of thing: 'forty is the new thirty'; 'poetry is the new comedy'; 'straight is the new gay'.) And yet it seems to me undeniable that at some point in the late 20th century self-pity became the new self-esteem — a situation that still continues today. 'Given the tendency to represent vulnerability as the defining feature of personhood,' writes Furedi in *On Tolerance*, 'it is not surprising that the identity of victim enjoys formidable cultural validation.'[13] Or here is Hughes in *Culture of Complaint*:

> The cult of the abused Inner Child has a very important use in modern America: it tells you that a personal grievance transcends political utterance, and that the upward production

curve of maudlin narcissism need not intersect with the
descending spiral of cultural triviality. Thus the pursuit of
the Inner Child has taken over just at the moment when
Americans ought to be figuring out where their Inner
Adult is, and how that disregarded oldster got buried under
the rubble of pop psychology and specious short-term
gratification. We imagine a Tahiti inside ourselves, and seek
its prelapsarian inhabitant: everyone his own Noble Savage.[14]

For Hughes, the 'claim to victimhood' can be staked
by anyone, including those whose biggest problem should
rightly be lower-back pain from so much time spent sitting
in the saddle. So when some men began to push back
against the feelings of guilt and powerlessness inflicted
on them by the women's movement, they often used the
techniques of consciousness-raising favoured by Hanisch
and her radical sisters. The 'mythopoets' of the 1980s —
most notably, Robert Bly — didn't stress their power over
women but rather the 'deep masculinity' that had been
repressed by over-dominant mothers.[15] According to this
logic, the modern man — cut off from nature, alienated
from his father, emotionally damaged by accusations of
sexism — was no less a victim of contemporary society
than the battered housewife. A covetous lust for the mantle
of victim is evident in such protestations. Underlying many
contemporary accusations of offence is a powerful sense of
victimhood. And underlying this sense of victimhood is
what could be described as 'trauma envy'.

This envy is also at play in the current appetite for celebrity memoirs that insist on the *brokenness* of their author-subjects. Writing in 2003, the British journalist Andrew O'Hagan expertly skewered this phenomenon: 'If you want to be somebody nowadays,' he wrote in the *London Review of Books*, 'you'd better start by getting in touch with your inner nobody, because nobody likes a somebody who can't prove they've been nobody all along.'[16] There was, he continued, a 'hummable, weepable, narcissistic self-pity' at large in such books, which, in bringing together the celebrity autobiography and the 'inspirational' misery memoir, invite their readers to part not only with their money, time, and admiration, but also with their sympathy. Or consider that most modern of literary forms, the *hoax* misery memoir. What could be more revealing of the phenomenon of trauma envy than Binjamin Wilkomirski's *Fragments*, an entirely fabricated account of a childhood spent in Majdanek and Auschwitz, or James Frey's *A Million Little Pieces*, a memoir of alcoholism and drug abuse exposed as a hoax in 2006? Such hoaxes are the personalised manifestations of the ideologically twisted histories treated in chapters two and three; stoking the furnace of victimhood, they build up a giant head of self-esteem. Thus self-pity takes its place at the centre of contemporary individualism. Or, as O'Hagan put it in his piece, employing his own 'new black' formulation, 'Pain is one of the new pleasures, abuse is the new nurturing.'

The Political Is Personal

There is a *pleasure* in victimhood, a thrill or buzz that those who indulge in it appear to crave and that the shock jocks, buffoonish media men, and populist pollies are happy to supply. Once again, Thomas Frank puts the matter vividly. Of those US conservatives who embraced the comparisons between the Obama administration and Nazi Germany, he paints the following psychological tableau:

> They tingled to imagine the outrageous injustices that would be done to them by the coming 'death panels'. They purred to hear about the campaign of 'indoctrination' that the new president had planned for their innocent kids; their pulse quickened to think of the 'chains' he was preparing for their mighty wrists; and they swelled with imagined bravery to picture how they would be targeted by 'the coming insurrection'.[17]

There is more than a touch of caricature in this sketch, but who can deny that Frank has identified a genuine, and genuinely odd, phenomenon? Some people clearly like feeling put upon; they want to feel ground down by power. Just as the would-be-celebrity memoirist enjoys the frisson afforded by trauma, so this modern political consumer is titillated by the thrill of victimhood. In expressing his anger, he compensates for it. He experiences affliction as an affirmation.

'Having displaced religion as the organising framework of American culture,' writes Lasch in *The Culture of Narcissism*, 'the therapeutic outlook threatens to displace politics as well, the last refuge of ideology.'[18] What we actually find, more than 30 years after Lasch committed that thought to paper, is not that therapy has displaced politics but that therapy and politics have, at some level, fused. Certainly politics has not disappeared: the terrorist attacks on New York and Washington on 11 September 2001 and the subsequent wars in Afghanistan and Iraq touched off a wide-ranging debate in the West about the reasons for Islamic terrorism and the US's neoconservative foreign policy, while climate change and the global financial crisis have refocused debate on the nature of capitalism and on the future of humankind itself. Ideas are big again — as evidenced by the recent popularity of such intellectuals and philosophers as John Gray, Slavoj Žižek, and David Harvey. But now the political is assumed to be personal. What we find in the early 21st century is a situation in which politics is experienced, increasingly if not predominantly, as an expression of individuality, albeit one that allows as well for the (sometimes dubious) satisfactions of group allegiance. The claim to political victimhood is only the most conspicuous symptom of this confusion between identity and belief, of the fact that emotionalism and politics have entered into a coalition whose slogan is 'I feel, therefore I am'.

I can't be the first to notice the way in which political protest now affords an opportunity for some people to show off their moral credentials (to ask, 'Does my conscience look big in this?'). In fact, I know I'm not the first because Ian McEwan noticed it brilliantly in his 2005 novel *Saturday*, which is set on the day of the massive march (in London, in February 2003) against the impending US-led invasion of Iraq. 'Not in My Name goes past a dozen times,' writes McEwan, referring to the ubiquitous slogan of the antiwar movement. 'Its cloying self-regard suggests a bright new world of protest, with the fussy consumers of shampoos and soft drinks demanding to feel good, or nice.'[19] Opposition to the war in Iraq was a perfectly honourable position to take, and many decent people took it; but while even adolescent slogans such as 'Give peace a chance' or 'Make love, not war' advance *some* kind of argument, 'Not in my name' suggests that a stance is valid by dint of its having been taken. Moreover, the slogan 'No Blood on My Hands' (also much in evidence in the antiwar protests of 2003) not only employed the personal pronoun, but also managed to mask the fact that what was at stake in the pre-war debate was a choice between two 'bloody' scenarios: a terrible war and a revolting dictator. The claim to personal innocence was an irrelevance at best. At worst, it was a sign that smug self-righteousness now passes for real political engagement.

This coming together of narcissism and allegiance is also demonstrated in the ubiquity of the 'awareness ribbon' and its close relation, the 'empathy wristband'. In her excellent study *Ribbon Culture*, Sarah Moore suggests that these adornments, while seeming to express solidarity, may actually work to undermine it. For Moore, such trinkets (which in the United States alone can now be worn for domestic violence, censorship, bullying, epilepsy, diabetes, brain cancer, chronic fatigue syndrome, autism, racial abuse, childhood disability, and mouth cancer, to name only a few) require neither knowledge of a particular cause nor a personal relationship with a sufferer. Appearing to signal concern for others, they in fact prioritise self-expression. Ribbon-wearing is about self-presentation, about 'making the self visible and readable'. But even as such displays increase, political engagement is on the wane: '"showing awareness" is a personal expression of annoyance, one that is generally very vague and always apolitical. The interest in displays of personal awareness reflects the decline of more traditional forms of political protest.'[20] The awareness ribbon and empathy wristband seem to answer to a modern need — a need to be seen to care about things — and to point towards a situation in which political beliefs are increasingly regarded not as meaningful intervention but as an expression of individuality. We desire the esteem that comes from allegiance but lack the will to act on it. In short, politics is increasingly a matter not of reasoned argument but of identification.

Because we experience politics personally, we take it personally when our politics are questioned. 'On some chthonic, pre-rational level,' writes Arthur Goldwag in *The New Hate*, 'many people — especially those who are already anxious about their shifting status — experience political criticism existentially, as a challenge to their very right to be the person they know themselves to be.'[21] Goldwag is talking predominantly about 'culture war' issues such as school prayer, guns, affirmative action, gay marriage, abortion, and euthanasia. But this 'pre-rational' mindset is now to be found in all areas of political discourse, with the result that even disagreements on issues such as climate change — ostensibly a highly technical matter — are characterised by anger and offendedness. In this situation, our political views are less reasoned responses to the world as it is, subject to change when the facts cease to support them, as they are expressions of personality. Consequently, a position becomes valid simply by dint of my having taken it. To invalidate it is to invalidate me, and thus excite my indignation. Again: I feel, therefore I am.

Epistemic Closure

In the past, Roman citizens would meet in the forum to ply their wares and exchange ideas. Today we often confuse the two, regarding ideas as something to 'try on', as accessories to self-expression. Moreover, the (metaphorical) forum in which our commentators used to do business has been looking increasingly shabby of late, vendors having moved to the outskirts of the city in order to cater to specific communities. And so the twilight of common dreams would seem to point to a bright new dawn in which people won't need to trouble themselves with the business of reasoned debate at all.

This process of intellectual atomisation is sometimes described as 'epistemic closure', a term that, thanks largely to Julian Sanchez of the libertarian Cato Institute in Washington, DC, has in recent years begun to take on a more specific political resonance. Sanchez uses 'epistemic closure' to describe the way in which some media outlets, particularly conservative outlets, can become dangerously untethered from reality. For Sanchez, himself a conservative, the fact that the media, though not consciously liberal, is reflective of broadly liberal attitudes, engenders a general suspicion of bias, to which the more conservative outlets respond by consciously trying to restore the balance. And so, while many networks and newspapers are *objectively* liberal, those of a more conservative bent tend to be *determinedly* rightwing — to the point where their approach appears less imbalanced than it does *un*balanced.[22]

One consequence of epistemic closure is thus a flight from reasoned debate, a cognitive withdrawal from the shared world of politics. This clearly has much in common with the phenomenon of cognitive dissonance identified by psychologist Leon Festinger in his 1956 study of UFO cult members *When Prophecy Fails*.[23] Festinger suggested that when facts that are contrary to a person's opinion emerge, that person often responds not by changing their views, but by proselytising for them even more fervently, as when the aliens stubbornly fail to arrive and the cult members take it as a sign of their own wisdom. Emphasising information that is consistent with their beliefs and avoiding information that isn't, they sacrifice truth to intellectual comfort.

As Clive Hamilton suggests in *Requiem for a Species*, this psychological process is at work in the thinking of many so-called climate change sceptics:

> If humans are rational creatures, we would expect that as the scientific evidence confirming human-induced global warming has become overwhelming, the deniers would adjust their beliefs to accommodate the facts. Yet they have become more vehement in their attacks on climate scientists, environmentalists and anyone who accepts the evidence for global warming.[24]

True. But why? Why, as Hamilton goes on to ask, do the sceptics *want* the science to be wrong, or appear to want the science to be wrong? After all, and unlike the UFO cult members tested in Festinger's study, no promise of everlasting happiness is involved in their being shown to be right. The answer, surely, is that Western politics is increasingly bound up with identity. The politics of identification leads first to denial and then to anger.

'Wherever there is uncertainty in the body of scientific evidence,' writes Hamilton, 'the deniers insert a crowbar into the chink and try to open up a crack that will bring the edifice down.'[25] It is not a new observation that modern technology, and the internet in particular, has vastly increased the leverage of those bent on such intellectual vandalism. Internet technology has catalysed a new, diverse world of knowledge, one aspect of which is the proliferation of extreme views and conspiracy theories.

Consequently, and paradoxically, the price of technological connectedness may turn out to be social disconnectedness. New technologies offer new opportunities to know more about the wider world, but they also allow us to limit our interactions to those who support our own ideas about society, culture, and politics.[26] This is not a new phenomenon; the futurologist Alvin Toffler noted something similar in *The Third Wave*. Yet it is clear that the internet has vastly accelerated the atomising process. In the era of the iPod, we now have iPolitics; we select those tracks that we are likely to warm to, pop in the earphones, and gently tap 'play'. 'Welcome to your world,' schmoozed *Time* magazine upon announcing that its 2006 Person of the Year was 'You'. (Its cover showed a computer screen, blank except for the personal pronoun.) But unless all us 'You's coalesce into a 'We' at some point down the road — unless we are able to come together and use the new technology to advance the cause of humanity — *Time*'s compliment to its readers will be undeserved.

If this sounds like an incontinent blast from Cassandra, reflect that when it comes to the internet there are plenty of Pollyannas, too. It is not uncommon to hear the proselytisers for Web 2.0 declare that it has the potential to bring the First Amendment to the whole of humanity. It's a bracing thought, and may even be true. But it's also true that internet technology vastly increases the opportunities for both giving and taking offence, and that it can engender an atmosphere that works against if not the letter then at least the spirit of freedom of speech. The social networking site Twitter connects people from all over the world, but since its creation in 2006 it has also served as an echo chamber for those who have an axe to grind. Taking offence at some newspaper article, or off-colour comment in an interview, or the musings of a fellow tweeter, the Twitter user is able to raise an instant mob. And so a technology that seems, on the face of it, to increase the scope for freedom of speech is frequently used to close it down. 'Like a modern-day version of those old medieval mobs that waved torches as they chased "witches",' writes the British journalist Brendan O'Neill, 'the Twittermob will demonise and try to squish anyone it deems to be a deviant … The 140-character tweet is the twenty-first-century equivalent of the rotten tomato.'[27]

Internet Rage

As Sanchez suggests in his definition of the term, such epistemic closure is in one sense a response to the openness of the internet. The scale and scope of the World Wide Web means that no one can control their audience or, indeed, predict its reaction. In conversation we might avoid views that are likely to offend those we're speaking to, but the internet makes this difficult, since our interlocutors are (potentially) in the billions. And while only a fool or a megalomaniac would imagine himself to be addressing those billions, that doesn't mean that some among them won't be offended by what we have to say. The problem is compounded by anonymity, which robs discussions of all those little tics and gestures that keep the majority of in-the-flesh disputes (and even telephone conversations) from descending into abuse or violence. A badly phrased blog post or comment or tweet is easily taken for a nasty one in the same way that an incompetent driver is easily taken for an obnoxious git.[28] It may even be that human beings are *naturally* uncomfortable debating in an anonymous environment. As a regular contributor to community blog *Less Wrong* puts it: '[W]e should consider the possibility that our offensiveness sense may be tuned too sensitively, perhaps for an ancestral environment where mass media didn't exist and any offence might reasonably be considered both personal and intentional.'[29]

Anonymity has another effect, of course, which is to allow those of us who take offence to vent our frustrations without fear of reprisal. It is now possible, upon taking offence, to dish it out with impunity. Psychologists call it 'deindividuation'— the shedding of social inhibition — and anyone who has followed the comments thread of an online political article knows precisely what the phenomenon entails: rudeness, sarcasm, bitterness, crassness, and, as Mike Godwin has pointed out, more Nazi analogies than you can shake a stick at.[30] Offendedness begets more offensiveness, which in turn begets more offendedness. And so on and so on, until skins are so thin and heads so thick with indignation that no one remembers how it all started or what the point of continuing is.

Writing in the United Kingdom's *Observer*, Tim Adams suggests that deindividuation has always been a problem on the internet. He cites the case of CommuniTree, a network of modem-linked computers set up in the 1970s, where pioneer dial-up internet users would convene to chat. Unfortunately, one of the institutions to which the network was linked was a high school, whose students, the pioneers quickly discovered, didn't share their high-minded ideals but were catching up rapidly in technical nous. Suddenly the network was flooded with abuse, four-letter words, and pornographic humour. Deciding that they could neither put up with the abuse nor bring themselves to censor it, CommuniTree's operators decided to fold.[31]

As Adams notes, this series of events is regarded as a kind of a 'founding myth' by those who seek to analyse the pros and cons of internet culture: 'It was one of the first moments when the possibilities of the new collective potential was tainted by anonymous lowest-common-denominator humanity, a pattern that has subsequently been repeated in pretty much all virtual communication.'[32] Certainly the internet does seem to have brought about a brave new world of abusiveness: the comments threads of online articles on anything from politics to celebrity gossip are apt to attract not only abuse but even detailed fantasies of violence. The internet 'troll' is now so ubiquitous that many websites now employ moderators or disallow anonymous comments altogether. A case in point is *3quarksdaily*, an indispensable daily digest of articles from around the planet, which recently lost patience with its nastier visitors and announced its intention to reject commentary it considers unnecessarily offensive.

In *The Offensive Internet*, Martha Nussbaum and Saul Levmore suggest that the internet is a lot like a village: it brings us together (whether we like it or not) and makes news and gossip available to all.[33] But while those who spread malicious gossip in a village may incur certain social costs, those who do so in an online environment are able to act with relative impunity. Similarly, a rioter in the flesh-and-blood world may be caught on closed-circuit television, but an online 'rioter' runs no such risk. Thus the internet invites not only the pleasures of political narcissism but also the pleasures of mob behaviour, and from the heady combination of the two emerges much antisocial conduct. Social-media sites such as Facebook and Myspace play host to all kinds of nastiness, not least the trolls who descend on pages dedicated to people who have died. It is not without significance that Facebook began as a program that allowed US university students to compare other students' looks. Facebook may be a 'social network', but antisocial attitudes and behaviour are written into its DNA.

None of this is to deny or downplay the massive benefits of the internet, which has opened up the world in a way that no other technology has managed to do. Nor is it to deplore the role of the pointed comment in political debate. It is merely to note that the internet is reflective of something deep in our culture — the personalisation of the political — and also proof (as if proof were needed) that the culture of sensitivity does not engender a more civil society but encourages its opposite. That is the central paradox of the politics of indignation, glimpsed in the revolting spectacle of a minor television personality being denounced as a 'slut' and a 'half-caste bitch' for a momentary lapse in judgement. Taking offence — and treating offence as something terrible in itself — we nonetheless grant ourselves leave to give it. To proscribe offence is not to build a Jerusalem of mutual respect, but to open the door to a Babel of complaint in which the loudest, nastiest voices prevail.

CHAPTER SEVEN

The Freedom to Offend

I cannot praise a fugitive and cloistered virtue, unexercised and unbreathed, that never sallies out and sees her adversary, but slinks out of the race where that immortal garland is to be run for, not without dust and heat.

JOHN MILTON, *AREOPAGITICA*

The Melbourne-based journalist Andrew Bolt is not an easy man to pity. Strident to the point of bumptiousness and tenacious to the point of fanaticism, not to mention unbendingly and noisily reactionary on issues ranging from immigration to religious values to multiculturalism, Bolt is the sort of conservative commentator who sends liberals staggering towards the fainting couch. But when, in March 2011, Bolt was sued by nine Australians under the *Racial Discrimination Act 1975* for suggesting that pale-skinned Aborigines have *chosen* to identify as Aboriginal (rather than as non- or part-Aboriginal) for reasons of personal and political advancement, he picked up some progressive sympathisers to add to his band of conservative admirers. Not because they agreed with his views on 'political Aborigines', of course, but because they thought the offending blog posts — 'It's So Hip to Be Black' and 'White Fellas in the Black' — fell within the realm of opinion and that, as such, it wasn't the role of men and women in horsehair wigs to say whether they were acceptable or not. To express it in the formula attributed (wrongly but plausibly) to Voltaire, the position of these progressives was, 'I disagree with what you say but will defend to the death your right to say it.' Moreover, many commentators were unnerved by the suggestion of Ron Merkel QC, leading the case for the prosecution, that Bolt's views on race bore a distinct resemblance to those that underwrote the 'science' of eugenics, as pursued by the Nazis in the 1940s. Certainly Bolt was angered by it. Appearing in the Federal Court in Melbourne on the second day of his eight-day trial, he was, according to witnesses, livid. 'It's not only false,' he said of Merkel's comparison, 'it's totally offensive.'

The language of offence is nothing if not catching, and Bolt is not to be pilloried for lapsing momentarily into it; after all, it isn't every day that one is accused of being a Nazi, even when one writes for the *Herald Sun*. But he makes a mistake if he thinks that his offendedness adds anything to the charge of falsity, or that the two things can be separated. In fact, the offensiveness of the Nazi comparison is inseparable from its falsity; the comparison is offensive *because* it is ridiculous, and any surplus feelings of offence are really neither here nor there. And while this may sound like pedantry, it is crucial to understanding the confusion — we might almost say the category mistake — that led to Bolt's appearance in court in the first place.

For although it emerged in the course of the trial that Bolt had been rather free with the facts, it is important to remember that it was not his fact-checking, or lack of it, for which he was standing trial, but his opinions about certain mixed-race Australians. Needless to say, the prosecution was happy to point to errors of fact, which they presented as evidence of the defendant's bad faith, and in his summing up Justice Mordecai Bromberg took these errors into consideration. But, again, and whatever Bolt's accusers in the Australian press and beyond it maintained, the conservative journalist was not in the dock for making false or defamatory statements but for contravening the Racial Discrimination Act, section 18C of which criminalises conduct 'reasonably likely … to offend, insult, humiliate or intimidate another person'. And on 28 September 2011 Justice Bromberg reached his verdict: Andrew Bolt was guilty as charged; guilty, that's to say, of the offence of offence.

A little over a year after that verdict was given, the Australian government released a draft of its proposed Human Rights and Anti-Discrimination Bill, the aim of which was to pull together several pieces of legislation into a more coherent and user-friendly package. This bill was the source of much debate, not least because it seemed to license a further extension of Australian law beyond the realm of checkable fact and into the shadowy lands of offence. In a piece on the ABC's website *The Drum*, the former Australian judge James Spigelman gave voice to this anxiety:

> Section 19(2)(b) of the proposed Human Rights and Anti-Discrimination Bill 2012, introduces 'offending' into the definition of discrimination for all purposes, not just for racial vilification. The new s19 defines, for the first time, discrimination by unfavourable treatment to include 'conduct that offends, insults or intimidates' another person. Significantly, unlike existing s18C … there is no element of objectivity, as presently found in the words 'reasonably likely to offend'. It appears to me the new bill contains *a subjective test of being offended*. [My italics.][1]

It hardly needs pointing out just how corrosive of any idea of vigorous, challenging, open debate 'a subjective test of being offended' would be if enshrined in Australian law, or indeed the law of any country. But that seems to be exactly where we're headed. Bolt's trial was not, as some maintained, a mere pimple on the body politic, but the symptom of a profound malaise, a malaise in which feelings of offence outweigh the proper presumption of freedom of speech. To reiterate: Bolt was *not* on trial for getting his facts wrong but for causing offence. Personally, I find that more offensive than the man himself — and that's saying something.

New laws (or new prosecutions under old ones) curtailing the right to freedom of opinion are not the principal subject of this book. But there is clearly a relationship between the culture of offence and respect, and the attempts to enshrine these concepts in law. That relationship is one of mutual reinforcement: the culture of offence and sensitivity leads to laws restricting freedom of expression, and laws restricting freedom of expression reinforce the culture of offence and sensitivity. Of course, it is easy to sound hysterical when discussing issues of free expression, and important to remember that, despite rightwing hyperbole, there is no *actual* Thought Police. But if the price of freedom is eternal vigilance, perhaps the price of eternal vigilance is (a little) hysteria. At any rate, there is no call for complacency.

As neither a philosopher nor a legal scholar, I'm not going to formulate a definitive defence of free speech in the pages that follow. But by rehearsing some of the arguments for it, I hope to press 'refresh' on a principle that many people choose to regard as some kind of Western luxury, and even as a manifestation of its laxity. That principle is essential — not only to our formal rights but also, and no less importantly, to the sense of ourselves as dignified beings, as thinking, respect-worthy members of society. I believe that a better acquaintance with the reasoning underlying the principle of free speech has the potential to engender more careful speech — that by reasserting the value of free speech, we can begin to disentangle ourselves from the thorny sensitivities now overgrowing our public spaces and ensure a higher *standard* of speech, going (as the pollies insist on saying) forward.

That Immortal Garland

But let us begin by going back 150 years or so and reacquainting ourselves with one of the key texts in the canon of free-speech literature. Published in 1859, John Stuart Mill's *On Liberty* suggests that free speech is the guarantor not only of individual happiness but also of societal health; without it, argues Mill, human society would not have been able to progress to its current, relatively sophisticated stage. By guaranteeing equal protection to those whose views are outside the mainstream (or beyond the pale), free speech ensures that what we call truth does not become the preserve of power. And by power Mill means not only the power of kings and priests and elected governments but also the power of the majority, which is just as capable of behaving tyrannically as the man with the crown or the surplice or the frock-coat. As he puts it, with appealing symmetry: 'If all mankind minus one were of one opinion ... mankind would be no more justified in silencing that one person than he, if he had the power, would be justified in silencing mankind.'[2]

Mill's reasoning is bracingly simple: the 'truth' is often not the truth, and those who presume to impose it upon everyone serve only to prevent the real truth from emerging.

To take the best-known example, for most of human history it was believed that the Sun moved around the Earth. Thanks largely to Copernicus and Galileo, we now know that this is not the case. Yet this view of our solar system would have taken hold more rapidly had it not been for the efforts of the Church to persecute its advocates and preserve the old Ptolemaic model, which had the advantage of placing man, supposedly God's greatest creation, at the centre of everything. By ensuring an exchange of views, free speech allows the truth to emerge. In Mill's words, it affords humanity 'the opportunity of exchanging error for truth'.[3]

Perhaps the best statement of this position is in the introduction to Thomas Paine's *The Age of Reason*. Published between 1794 and 1807, this spirited pamphlet subjected organised Christianity to criticism and often vulgar ridicule; as such, it ran the risk of censure in those countries where it was likely to be read. Addressing himself to the only country to offer some protections in this regard, the English-born activist and political theorist put the case for free speech like this:

TO MY FELLOW-CITIZENS OF THE UNITED STATES OF AMERICA:
I put the following work under your protection. It contains my opinions upon Religion. You will do me the justice to remember, that I have always strenuously supported the Right of every Man to his own opinion, however different that opinion might be to mine. He who denies to another

> this right, makes a slave of himself to his present opinion, because he precludes himself the right of changing it.
>
> The most formidable weapon against errors of every kind is Reason. I have never used any other, and I trust I never shall.
>
> > Your affectionate friend and fellow-citizen,
> > THOMAS PAINE[4]

The sentence beginning 'He who denies to another this right' is Mill's position in a nutshell; free speech protects not only the speaker but also the community of potential hearers and readers (including the censor himself), whose pursuit of the truth is impeded by not being exposed to it.

Furthermore, in proscribing certain views we lose the intellectual muscles needed to defend our own. As any writer can attest, the mind, no less than the biceps and triceps, is apt to atrophy if underused, and it behoves the intellectual competitor to train in the Gym of the Taken-for-Granted before taking to the Stadium of Finer Points where the 'immortal garland' (as John Milton described it) of 'virtue' is competed for. Recently, I sat in on the trial of a Perth man accused of racial hatred. When passing sentence, the presiding judge, referring to the video in which the defendant had made the offending comments, described the man's views (which revolved around a loathing for Israel, and the Jewish people more generally) as 'self-evidently ridiculous'. In doing so, he told an obvious untruth (if the man's opinions were self-evidently ridiculous, he and his sympathisers wouldn't have held them) and managed to turn the opposing opinion into a formulaic and unthinking response. This was Mill's second point: by asking the state to enforce a conclusion to which we have come at some previous time, or to which society has come on our behalf, we abdicate responsibility; we neither disabuse anyone of a wrongheaded view nor remind ourselves of why we regard a particular view as wrongheaded in the first place. To abolish certain attitudes is to invite intellectual laziness, to turn living beliefs into dead dogma.

Consider David Irving, the British historian whose denial of the Holocaust led to his imprisonment in Austria in November 2005. The result of this disgraceful episode was that Irving became a free-speech martyr, a mantle that served to (partially) obscure his jackboots. By contrast, when Irving attempted to sue the author Deborah Lipstadt and her publishers for libel in 1996, those boots became more conspicuous, not less. Obliged to disprove the argument Lipstadt had made in *Denying the Holocaust* — namely, that he had fiddled the evidence in pursuit of his eccentric reading of history — Irving was forced to publicise his views as well as his flawed methodology, and such reputation as he had came unravelling quicker than a ball of wool under attack from a litter of kittens. A key element of the Lipstadt case was a report compiled by Richard Evans, a professor of modern history at Cambridge. Irving, said Evans, had distorted facts and mistranslated documents. He concluded: 'Irving has fallen so far short of the standards of scholarship customary among historians that he does not deserve to be called a historian at all.'[5] The result was that Irving lost his case. More to the point, he lost the argument.

Irving's imprisonment in Austria occurred not long after the Danish cartoons controversy, and it also highlighted another problem stemming from attempts to curtail free speech — the way in which, in banning an opinion, we make a rod for our own backs. Many Muslims were only too happy to point out the hypocrisy of inhibiting Irving's freedom of speech while defending European newspapers' right to print the Muhammad cartoons. Certainly the secretary-general of the Arab League wasted no time in pointing out the double standard: 'What about freedom of expression when anti-Semitism is involved?' Amr Moussa asked. 'Then it is not freedom of expression. Then it is a crime. Yet when Islam is insulted, certain powers raise the issue of freedom of expression.'[6] To condemn an opinion is to prepare the ground for further condemnations of opinion in the future. For who will deny that on questions of principle, slopes are always slippery? A principle, after all, is only valid if it applies to all cases equally; and the principle underlying freedom of speech is that it must include the freedom to offend.

Offence as Harm

Having said that, even free-speech advocates recognise the need for *some* restrictions on what can be said in the public sphere. Few, for example, would countenance slander or highly misleading advertising. The question is where to draw the line — or, more accurately, *how* to draw the line in a way that ensures that exceptions to the presumption of free speech are really exceptions and not the preamble to less desirable encroachments.

The answer given by Oliver Wendell Holmes Jr, an associate justice of the US Supreme Court from 1902 to 1932, is that freedom of speech should not extend to 'falsely shouting fire in a theatre and causing a panic'.[7] This hoary analogy is ever on the lips of prime ministers and home secretaries called upon to justify, say, an extension of the hate-speech laws, or the refusal of a temporary visa to some nasty little demagogue of the 'Islam Is an Evil Religion' school (or, indeed, some tedious mullah of the 'Freedom Go to Hell' madrasa.) Yet given the analogy's provenance, its ubiquity is hard to fathom. For the case on which Holmes happened to be ruling when these words found their way through his imperial moustache had nothing to do with shouting fire but with a Yiddish-speaking socialist who'd distributed an anti-conscription leaflet to military draftees in 1919. The socialist was being sent to jail not for causing a stampede on Broadway but for protesting against US involvement in World War I! It is often, quite legitimately, asked of those who would place limits on freedom of expression: 'Who would you trust to decide what is and what is not acceptable speech?' On the strength of his most famous statement, I wouldn't trust Justice Holmes.

A better argument is made by those who claim to have identified a central weakness in Mill's position: his underlying assumption that all speech is about the search for truth. To read some scholars who advocate for freedom of speech is to be transported to a peculiar realm where opinions are exchanged like crackers at Christmas. 'Free speech is a condition of legitimate government,' writes the US philosopher Ronald Dworkin. 'Laws and policies are not legitimate unless they have been adopted through a democratic process, and a process is not democratic if government has prevented anyone from expressing his convictions about what those laws and policies should be.'[8] Such adamantine logic is hard to fault, though it is just as hard to suppress the suspicion (because the logic *is* so adamantine) that Dworkin is leaving something out. And that something is to be found, I think, behind the phrase 'expressing his convictions'— a noble-sounding enterprise, but one that conceals some ignoble conduct.

For the fact is that in 'expressing our convictions' we might just be expressing our contempt or hatred, and that those on whom the contempt or hatred happens to be concentrated might feel that some harm is being done to them — that they are being attacked in their deepest dignity. Mill believed that humans should be free to do whatever they wanted, so long as they didn't harm anyone in the process. But he was talking about *physical* harm, not the kind of mental harm that may result from an attack on someone's identity. 'Sticks and stones may break my bones,' the children's nursery rhyme runs, 'but names will never hurt me.' Not so, reply the enemies of hate speech; words can cut as deeply as any weapon. Why should shoving a gay person be regarded as an assault on their personhood but calling them a 'faggot' not?

It's an excellent question, but in attempting to answer it we need to tread very carefully. Political correctness has led to an expansion of the meaning of 'harm' that should strike free-speech advocates as potentially disastrous. The US feminist Catharine MacKinnon was one of the drivers of this development. Her view, which she formulated with reference to the work of the British philosopher J. L. Austin, was that many words or sentiments are essentially indistinguishable from deeds, and that sexist or misogynistic language should be regarded as a species of violence.[9] This led to a notion of 'assaultive' speech that is now a lot less controversial than it should be, and it's easy to see how problems would arise if such a concept was enshrined in law: the distinction between hurting someone's feelings and hurting them physically would become dangerously blurred.

In his famous, and famously controversial, essay 'There's No Such Thing as Free Speech and It's a Good Thing, Too', the US scholar Stanley Fish attempts to triumph over this 'slippery slope' argument by affecting to skip to the top of the hill and ride his philosophical tea-tray, legs akimbo, all the way down it. He takes as his launching point for this reason-defying stunt John Milton's great defence of free speech, *Areopagitica* (named, appropriately, for the hill that functioned as the court of appeal in ancient Athens). This makes it an especially thrilling spectacle, and may even sanction a sneaking suspicion that the Davidson-Kahn Distinguished University Professor of Humanities and Law is, well, showing off a bit. At any rate, in taking issue in so bold a way with so great a thinker, Fish gives an inadvertent demonstration of just how intellectually perilous the confusion of speech with action can be.

Fish's stated objective is to defend university campus codes against those critics of both the left and the right who regard them as an assault on the very principles around which the university should be organised. Milton's *Areopagitica* argues that truth is the object of mankind's continuing quest and that it is not the property of any one church. Unfortunately, Milton lets himself down when he says that this doesn't apply to Roman Catholicism, for that which is 'impious or evil absolutely against faith or manners no law can possibly permit that intends not to unlaw itself'.[10] This exception, says Fish, might appear 'ad hoc and unprincipled', but in fact it operates as a kind of theoretical boundary without which Milton's notion of free expression ceases to have any definition.[11] In other words, Milton's defence of free speech only holds water on account of the passage that free-speech advocates are usually invited to regard as a stain on an otherwise spotless argument. Moreover, says Fish, '*all affirmations* [my italics] of freedom of expression are like Milton's, dependent for their force on an exception that literally carves out the space in which expression can then emerge'.[12] What is this exception? For Fish, the answer is that category of speech referred to in the

US Constitution as 'fighting words': words that are liable to incite either violence or a breach of the peace. And for Fish, this category of speech is a lot more 'capacious' than is usually recognised; he argues that since all utterances are (potentially) an incitement to *somebody*, there is actually no such thing as free speech. As he puts it:

> I mean that there is no class of utterances separable from the world of conduct, no 'merely' cognitive expressions whose effects can be confined to some prophylactically sealed area of public discourse. And since it is just such expressions that are privileged by the First Amendment … there is nothing for the amendment to protect, no items in the category 'free expression'.[13]

And so, having provided the philosophical justification for that 'subjective test of being offended' so (rightly) feared by Judge Spigelman, Fish proposes to ban 'hate speech' — a category, if one follows his logic, as limitless as speech itself. The reason for this, he tells us, is that 'at the present moment, right now, the risk of not attending to hate speech is greater than the risk that by regulating it we will deprive ourselves of valuable voices and insights or slide down the slippery slope toward tyranny'.[14] By which brilliant bit of sophistry Fish earns himself admission to the club (chairman: Oliver Wendell Holmes Jr) for people to whom nothing of importance should ever be entrusted. Ever!

'Harm' as Subjective

I'm not denying the psychic pain that abusive and hateful language can inflict. But to conflate offence and actual harm is to land ourselves in serious trouble. The *insult* visited upon the Jewish people by those who deny the Holocaust may compound the *injury* caused by the event itself; but the insult is not *identical* with the injury, and any suggestion otherwise is an invitation to censorship. The sentiment 'The right to swing my fist ends where the other man's nose begins' is common in discussions about free speech. But in using violence as a metaphor for human communication, this dictum gives a decisive head start to the very confusion I'm determined to resist: the confusion between offence and (physical) harm. Unless the distinction is vigilantly maintained, we will end up in a situation in which the clamour for 'respect' and 'dignity' trounces the presumption to free expression.

For the fact is, offence is a two-way street on which the signage is all over the place. Unlike issues of physical violence, where particular actions can be deemed to have occurred and to have resulted in particular consequences, the concept of offence is partly subjective. If I punch you in the face and break your nose, your broken nose is an objective fact. But if I say that I don't like your face, your feelings of hurt will be peculiar to you, if they exist at all. This element of subjectivity is inherent in the notion of offence. To *commit* an offence is to perform an action, the seriousness of which is determined by law; to *give* offence is to perform an action — or, more usually, make a statement — the seriousness of which is partly dependent on someone else's interpretation of it. Citing the *Oxford English Dictionary*'s second definition of offence, which reads, 'The act of offending, wounding the feelings of, or displeasing another; usually viewed as it affects the person offended', Stefan Collini puts the matter cogently:

> First, the emphasis is on the subjectivity of the person offended; and second, offence exists principally in the sphere of the feelings. Taken together, these two characteristics may suggest that if someone does not feel offended, then they have not been offended. And this may in turn seem to entail the reverse proposition, namely that each individual is the only possible judge of whether or not they have been offended.[15]

To be clear, Collini's argument is not that people don't offend others, nor that they do not set out to do so, but that this element of subjectivity means that attempts to enforce respect are always subject to mission creep. Broken noses are one thing; hurt feelings, another.

Indignation and Dignity

Many advocates of free-speech restrictions, aware of the subjective nature of offence, have formulated or attempted to formulate objective notions of human dignity, which could act as a touchstone in the arguments about the limits of acceptable speech. The philosopher Jeremy Waldron is one such. In his 2012 book *The Harm in Hate Speech*, he argues that since the aim of hate speech is to 'compromise the dignity of those at whom it is targeted', it should be subject to certain restrictions. As he puts it, 'public order means more than just the absence of fighting: it includes the peaceful order of civil society and the dignitary order of ordinary people interacting with one another in ordinary ways … on the basis of arm's-length respect.' The problem, of course, is how to define dignity, and for that the professor leans heavily on the case of *Beauharnais v. Illinois* (1952), when the US Supreme Court upheld the constitutionality of an Illinois statute prohibiting any material that portrayed 'depravity, criminality, unchastity, or lack of virtue of a class of citizens, of any race, colour, creed or religion'. This is clearly the kind of thing that Waldron would like to see adopted generally: in his view, those who attack what he calls the 'basic social standing and reputation of a group' should be deemed to have trespassed on the dignity of that group and thus be subject to prosecution.[16]

For Waldron, an individual's 'membership' of a particular group is not to be muddled up with that individual's beliefs; his argument is that restrictions on hate speech should be aimed at preventing attacks on dignity and not at merely offensive viewpoints. So presumably I could say, if I wanted to, 'Christianity is an evil religion', but not 'Christians are evil people' — a distinction I'm prepared to accept as crucial, even though I think I should be able to say both. But in mapping group-membership so intimately into his formulation of dignity, Waldron flirts with the mindset we've come to associate with identity politics, which is apt to put the dignity of the group before the dignity of its individual members.

Moreover, the habit of thinking of ourselves as members of a particular group is itself potentially corrosive of dignity. As George Kateb, a professor of politics at Princeton University, puts it,

> [I]f a person thinks of himself or herself first as a member of a group, that person has defined identity as affiliation, and not as first being oneself. To be affiliated with one's whole self is to welcome docility, to endorse the thought that one's possibilities are exhausted, perhaps from birth, and that one cannot change or be changed.[17]

A state that seeks to protect its citizens against what Waldron calls 'group defamation' seems to me to run the risk of infantilising those citizens, of undermining their dignity, by assuming that they can't stick up for themselves. That arguments for curtailing freedom of speech are so often made with reference to children is in this sense a worrying sign, since children are citizens without full autonomy.

Again, I am not saying that bigoted speech is something to be taken lightly. But to ban such speech is not only to encourage prohibitions of the MacKinnon–Fish variety; it is also corrosive in itself of a particular idea of human dignity as resting on our capacity for reason and argument.

As Collini writes in *That's Offensive!*, 'the most important identity we can acknowledge in another person is the identity of being an intelligent reflective human being'.[18] We may feel that our dignity is undermined by those who demean our race or gender, but it is further undermined when the state (or the university) assumes the right and responsibility of conducting arguments on our behalf.

Not Without Dust and Heat

Professor Fish is right about one thing: the idea of free speech depends for its efficacy on some limiting case or set of cases that illuminate the principle underlying it. But he is wrong to argue that 'fighting words' reveal that underlying principle to be responsible, non-inciting speech; and he is also disingenuous to argue that since all words are in some sense 'fighting', the notion of free speech is self-negating. For the principle underlying the First Amendment — the reason for its having been framed at all — is, as Mill saw, the 'search for truth'. That is why the US Constitution does not permit defamation or fraud: because demonstrably false or misleading claims about people or products are rightly regarded as corrosive of the very search for truth that free speech seeks to protect and encourage. It is also the reason, as Fish must know, there exists an injunction against fighting words, which is to say against direct incitement. Clearly, someone who solicits violence is not engaged in truth-seeking behaviour; he is trying to effect damage to people or property. The problem, as we've seen, occurs when it comes to the notion of hurtful speech. For if I claim, as I never would, that homosexuality is an abomination, who is to say whether this is the legitimate opinion of a truth-seeking individual, or an expression of hate, or a bit of both? The whole notion of hate speech is problematic in this way, asking us to choose between the liberty of the (offending) speaker and the equality of the (offended) hearer. I think the emphasis should fall on the first thing, for the simple and sufficient reason that to sacrifice liberty for equality is to ensure that eventually you'll end up with neither.

'More heat than light' is a resonant phrase, but also a misleading one. For clearly there can be no light without heat, no illumination without argument, no immortal garland without the race. *Of course* it's painful to be told to your face that your beliefs are wishful thinking, that your prophets and messiahs are peddlers of pure hokum, or that you and your kind are silly or inferior. But agreeability is not synonymous with emancipation, or even a prerequisite for it. 'An honest man speaks the truth, though it may give offence,' wrote William Hazlitt, 'a vain man, in order that it may.'[19] True enough, but we make a big mistake if we think that we can have the honesty without the vanity, or the dignity without the freedom to think.

This is not to argue that to publish a nasty article on 'political Aborigines' is a dignified act: to say that the capacity for reasoned argument gives human beings dignity — or is among the things that give them dignity

— is not to say that dignity and reasoned argument are identical. The point is that the imperatives of 'respect' are not always compatible with intellectual combativeness, and so with intellectual progress. Such progress is born *of* strenuous conflict, not in spite of it. Tolerance is not the same as acceptance, which is a kind of intellectual charity; tolerance is the precondition for disagreement.[20] It does not guarantee equality, but it does clear a space in which the idea of equality can be argued over, and we encroach upon that space at our peril. For while many offensive things will be said in that argument about equality nothing is to be gained from disengagement. The claim to find something hurtful or offensive should be the beginning of the debate, not the end of it. That, as far as *this* debate goes, is surely the beginning of wisdom.

Is Nothing Sacred?

The best lack all conviction, while the worst
Are full of passionate intensity.
W.B. YEATS, 'THE SECOND COMING'

When I first viewed the footage on YouTube, almost exactly halfway through the writing of this book, it occurred to me that I must be watching a version of the movie trailer cobbled together by some enterprising pornographer, or that students in thrall to Monty Python had contrived to use the controversy surrounding it as an excuse to pay homage to their comedy heroes. Surely, I thought, *this* can't be it. But as the seconds elapsed (and the will to live ebbed) it became apparent that the clumsy dubbing, spray tans, fake beards, and transcendentally bad acting were only the outward manifestations of a crude attack on the Islamic religion, and on its prophet in particular.

Against an unrealistic desert backdrop, the calumnies come thick and fast: Muhammad was a halfwit who conversed with donkeys; Muhammad was a tyrant who tortured old ladies; Muhammad was a drunk and a sexual predator who slept with boys as well as women. ('Is our leader dominant or submissive?' asks a follower. 'Both!' declares a sozzled Proph.) 'Man plus X equals Islamic terrorist,' says a character at the top of the film, adding, no less seemingly enigmatically, 'Islamic terrorist minus X equals man.' The speaker is a Coptic Christian whose business has just been trashed by Muslims, and though he declines to tell us what X is, it is fairly clear that it stands for Muhammad. The imputation is that Islam is a religion not of peace but of lethal violence — that violence is in its DNA. Still, it's not all seriousness and solemnity; for example, in the penultimate scene, God's messenger is depicted trying to outpace two of his more jealous wives, having been discovered *in flagrante* with a (female) servant.

The film's quality is hardly the point, of course. That *The Innocence of Muslims*, as it has since become known, combines the pomposity of religious epic with the production values of *Invaders from Mars* and the narrative arc of *The Benny Hill Show* was less important to those who objected to it than the fact that the film was made at all: yet another illustration of the utter contempt with which the West regards Islam and its injunctions against depicting the Prophet. Nevertheless, when Mark Basseley Youssef, an Egyptian-born Coptic Christian based in California, released the footage in September 2011, the juxtaposition of one of the dumbest films ever made and the orgy of violent protest it caused — with rallies being held across the 'Muslim world'— did serve to concentrate the mind on the inevitably subjective nature of offence. From Egypt to Yemen to India to Pakistan to Indonesia to Australia, the crowds pronounced sentence of death on the infidel; *fatwas* were issued, bounties raised, and an estimated 50 people killed in violence. And for what? This 15 minutes of drivel.

So striking was this disconnection that a new mood seemed momentarily to take hold across the media and political landscape. For amid all the usual chants and placards — 'Death to Freedom and Democracy'; 'Obama, Obama, We Love Osama'; 'Behead Those Who Insult the Prophet' (this last held aloft by a three-year-old boy in Sydney's central business district) — one group was conspicuous by its quietness: the community of commentators who can usually be relied upon, when the political weather turns inclement, to shake their heads and pull a face and say that while freedom of speech is important, those who engage in irresponsible speech are at least partly to blame for whatever mayhem happens to be engulfing our screens. Of course, there were politicians and churchmen on hand to deplore the video. ('To us, to me personally,' said Hillary Clinton, 'this video is disgusting and reprehensible.' The film, declared the World Council of Churches, was 'an insult to all peoples of faith'.) But there was very little from the commentariat. No doubt this had to do with the fact that in order to make excuses for something, you need to have something to excuse it with. A magical-realist novel will serve; cartoons in a right-wing newspaper are better. But a self-satirising slice of tripe served up on a video-sharing website — the 'trailer' for a movie that may not exist and, if it does, has apparently been shown only once, in a rented cinema in California to an invited audience of less than ten people? This was impossible to take seriously. And so to engage in the usual apologetics would have been to make yourself ridiculous, like an actor wrestling a rubber crocodile. Of course, there was always the fallback position whereby you claimed that the demonstrators were 'really' angry about something else; that Palestine, say, or the war in Iraq was the 'real' issue, not blasphemy. And yet, with each new controversy, the returns on this argument necessarily diminish. After all, blasphemy, and not Palestine or Iraq, is the issue on which the protestors settled, and have settled many times before. Sooner or later the thought begins to form that perhaps, just *perhaps*, the noisy constituency laying waste to a cinema in Peshawar or defacing a US flag in Chennai or hurling bottles at policemen in Sydney is really as ridiculous and unreasonable as it looks.

This new mood didn't last for long. A few days into the video controversy, a French weekly satirical newspaper with a strongly anti-clerical stance decided to enter the fray with a vengeance. A home to scruffy leftwingers and anarchists, and an abattoir for sacred cows, *Charlie Hebdo*'s contribution to the debate was to produce an issue containing a number of caricatures of Muhammad in the all-together.[1] On its cover was a cartoon of an orthodox

Jew pushing a Muslim in a wheelchair and the headline 'The Intouchables 2', an allusion to the syrupy flick which was at that time taking France by storm. The stunt was scarcely more high-minded than the one that touched off the wider furore, but at least the fact that *Charlie*'s staff are sophisticated media types allowed the usual suspects to revert to their line that Muslim rage is the symptom of the many indignities visited upon Islam by the West. No doubt this opinion took some hits in the week leading up to *Charlie*'s intervention. After it, normal service resumed.[2]

Such tentativeness on a point of principle is not an isolated phenomenon. It is but one, rather passive, manifestation of a culture in which complaint gives you power — a culture in which we take the wish for the reality, and take offence when reality doesn't measure up to the wish. In a sense, the apologists mirror the faithful. The young men laying waste to that cinema are doing so because they claim to know that God's wishes are inscribed in a particular text; and the commentators making apologies for them or asking us to share our blame around are doing so because they believe that a person's 'identity' is sacrosanct. The first group seeks to ban the subversive, the second group to suppress the offensive. But both are making essentially the same point, which they are apt to put in the form of a question. That question is, 'Is nothing sacred?' And my answer to that — as you might guess — is 'no'.

This is *my* faith, but it is a faith that admits of all other faiths, except those that would take away my right to criticise them. When that right is challenged, I too experience indignation, and that indignation comes wrapped in the thought that in attempting to shrink the intellectual space in which convictions (and even prejudices) are exchanged, we are simply preparing the ground for more conflict. Politics, like nature, abhors a vacuum, and if the people in my ideological constituency are unwilling to criticise religious extremists, there are plenty of people at the other end of the political spectrum who are happy to do so, in terms that it would be effete to describe as unhelpful to the tone of the debate. Rumours in the Australian press that the anti–*Innocence of Muslims* protests would be met by a thuggish response on the streets turned out to be just that — rumours. But there is a palpable sense that such a confrontation has merely been postponed. Offence begets yet more offence, identities yet more identities. And what is fascism, after all, if not identity politics in uniform?

As someone who makes his living from words, there are two things about which I feel qualified, as opposed to just entitled, to comment. The first is freedom of opinion and expression, which I regard as an 'unalienable' right, to be defended at all costs and on all fronts. And the second is the abuse of that right by people in the public sphere. To those who say that the second thing is made more likely by my adherence to the first, I respond that the opposite case holds true — that it is only by *valuing* freedom of speech that its nastier manifestations can be properly countered. To be clear: I am offended *all the time* — by racism, by demagoguery, and above all, by bullies. But I would no more demand the right *not* to be offended than I would the right to own a machine gun. To do that would be to concede that the argument was simply too hard or too upsetting to have, or too obvious to bother making. In short, it would be to admit defeat, or to assume a victory in advance of one, and make everyone else hostage to my feelings.

Easy for me to say, I know. And it is true that such things as offend me are rarely aimed directly at me, a white man living in a predominantly white country, subject to nothing more upsetting than the occasional abusive email or sarcastic retort in the comments section. Moreover (it could be reasonably said), not everyone has the inclination or the skills to argue with their political enemies. In response to the first objection, I can only reiterate the point made in the last chapter: that those who would exchange their liberty for equality will end up undermining both. As for the second, I stand with Mill in believing that a healthy polity *demands* that kind of civic engagement, and that what goes for the muscles goes as well for minds: without exercise they will atrophy. Only by challenging bigots and haters can we build a society from which, in the long run, bigots and haters are less likely to emerge.

This is surely the key point. For it is not as if the culture of offendedness is in any sense relatable to some sharp up-tick in political civility; on the contrary, incivility prevails in the current political scene. Rabblerousers are ten a penny, and the rabble as willing as ever to be roused.

The paradox is as plain as day and makes the case all by itself: to insist on respect and sensitivity is not to build a kinder society but one in which frustrations multiply and fester.

Even if this were not the case — even if it could be demonstrated that the proscription of offence was good for public discourse — we would still be faced with a situation in which a trader sitting at his desk in New York can offend a mobile-phone salesman in Jakarta in less time than it takes to unwrap a stick of gum. 'Globalised world' may be a tautology, but it seems to be a necessary one, describing a technological, as well as an economic, reality. Pastor Terry Jones, who we met in Chapter 1, and Mark Basseley Youssef are merely point men in an invisible army of zealots, vandals, bigots, and bigmouths who get their kicks by abusing others. Depressing it may be, but they have a right to make fools of themselves. We had better get used to defending that right, and to saying why we think they're fools — and to saying why those who respond to them with violence and bigotry and demands for censorship are foolish, too.

Notes

Introduction: The Mind on Fire

1 In fact, a number of conservative commentators had taken 'Cordoba House' to be a triumphalist reference to the Islamic conquest of Spain in the eighth century.

2 John Dickerson, 'Taking Offense Is the Best Offense', *Slate*, 25 February 2008. One of the most telling controversies involved the case of the *New Yorker* front cover that depicted Senator Barack Obama in a turban and Muslim-style tunic and trousers, and the future First Lady in camouflage pants and with an AK-47 slung across her back. Clearly, the magazine's intention was to satirise the anti-Obama hysteria forming at the edges of the populist right. But Obama's 'people' didn't see the joke, or at any rate affected not to. Not to be outdone in the indignation stakes, Senator McCain's political team also issued a statement deploring the image.

3 An example: on 11 April 2011, Bess Price, an Aboriginal activist, appeared on the ABC's *Q&A* program, in the course of which she defended the Howard government's controversial Northern Territory intervention. Seeing this, Larissa Behrendt, an Aboriginal academic and opponent of said intervention, made the following comment on Twitter: 'I watched a show where a guy had sex with a horse and I'm sure it was less offensive than Bess Price'. Offended by Behrendt's offendedness, or at least by the terms in which it was couched, Price considered legal action, while the federal Shadow Minister for Indigenous Affairs said that he was 'appalled' by the comment. (Price's husband went one better, describing it as an 'obscene vilification'.) Claiming that the tweet had been taken out of context, Behrendt nevertheless apologised, though sections of the conservative press seemed reluctant to let her off the hook. One reason for this, it's pretty clear, is that Behrendt

had recently appeared as a witness in the case against columnist Andrew Bolt, who was being sued by nine Australians under the Racial Discrimination Act for suggesting that pale-skinned Aborigines have *chosen* to identify as Aboriginal rather than as non- or part-Aboriginal. More on that in Chapter Seven.

4   Tim Adams, 'How the Internet Created an Age of Rage', *The Observer*, 24 July 2011.

5   Benet Davetian, *Civility: a cultural history*, University of Toronto Press, Toronto, 2009.

Chapter One: When Dawkins Met Haggard

1   Frans de Waal, *Primates and Philosophers: how morality evolved*, Princeton University Press, Princeton, 2006, p. 4.

2   ibid., p. 8.

3   Adam Smith, *The Theory of Moral Sentiments* (1759), Cambridge University Press, Cambridge, 2002, p. 135.

4   Charles Darwin, *The Descent of Man*, John Murray, London, 1871, p. 103.

5   It follows that some non-human animals will also display sympathetic behaviour — a point de Waal illustrates beautifully with the story of a chimpanzee attempting to help an injured bird take flight.

6   Christopher Boehm, *Moral Origins: the evolution of virtue, altruism, and shame*, Basic Books, New York, 2012, p. 319.

7   Richard Dawkins, *The God Delusion*, Bantam Press, Sydney, 2006, p. 217.

8   See de Waal, op. cit., pp. 17–20.

9   Smith, op. cit.

10 Margaret Atwood, *Payback: debt and the shadow side of wealth*, Bloomsbury, London, 2008, p. 13.

11 ibid., p. 19.

12 See Emily Yoffe, 'Well, Excuuuuuse Meee!', *Slate*, 17 October 2008.

13 ibid.

14 For the full discussion, see Wei_Dai, 'The Nature of Offense', *Less Wrong*, http://lesswrong.com/lw/13s/the_nature_of_offense

15 Jonathan Haidt, 'Moral Psychology and the Misunderstanding of Religion', *Edge*, 21 September 2007.

16 Irena Maryniak, *Offence: the Christian case*, Seagull Books, Kolkata, 2009, p. 26.

17 In Dawkins, op. cit., pp. 228–229.

18 A. C. Grayling, *Towards the Light: the story of the struggles for liberty and rights that made the modern West*, Bloomsbury, New York, 2007, p. 23.

19 Christopher Hitchens, *God Is Not Great: how religion poisons everything*, Allen & Unwin, Sydney, 2007.

20 A. C. Grayling, *Liberty in the Age of Terror: a defence of civil liberties and Enlightenment values*, Bloomsbury, New York, 2009.

21 Grayling, *Towards the Light*, op. cit., p. 59.

22 Davetian, op. cit., p. 160.

23 ibid., p. 225.

24 Lady Troubridge, *The Book of Etiquette*, The World's Work, Kingswood, 1958, p. 1.

25 This reminds me of Wyndham Lewis' observation, quoted by George Orwell, that the English working classes are 'branded on the tongue'.

26 G. K. Chesterton, *Essays and Poems*, Penguin, London, 1958, pp. 168–179.

27 Timothy Garton Ash, 'Living with Difference', *Free Speech Debate*, 22 January 2012, freespeechdebate.com.

28 Steven Pinker, *The Stuff of Thought: language as a window into human nature*, Viking, New York, 2007, pp. 323–373.

29 See in particular Professor Jonathan Miller's lecture on humour for *QED*, available on YouTube.

30 Joel Warner, 'One Professor's Attempt to Explain Every Joke Ever', *Wired*, 26 April 2011.

Chapter Two: From Enlightenment to Entitlement

1 In order to get around the ban on public address systems imposed by the authorities, organisers employed the 'people's mic', by which people sitting near the front of the crowd would repeat, and thus amplify, each speaker's words. To keep noise to a minimum, protesters communicated with the speakers or invigilators through a series of hand signals; an upward 'twinkling' of the fingers, for example, registered agreement with whoever was speaking.

2 Writers for the 99%, *Occupying Wall Street: the inside story of an action that changed America*, Scribe Publications, Melbourne, 2012, p. 121.

3 ibid., p. 111.

4 ibid., p. 112.

5 See for example 'OWS — Where Does Feminism Fit?', *Care2*, 22 November 2011, www.care2.com.

6 'One Year Later: Occupy in disarray but spirit lives on', *CBSNews*, 16 September 2012.

7 Thomas H. Naylor, 'Who Is Occupying Whom?', *Counterpunch*, 27 March 2012.

8 Henry Hitchings, *The Language Wars: a history of proper English*, John Murray, London, 2011, p. 235.

9 Alexis de Tocqueville, *Democracy in America*, vol. II, Longman, London, 1862, p. 146.

10 Martin Amis, *The War against Cliché: essays and reviews 1971–2000*, Jonathan Cape, London, 2001, pp. 164–65.

11 In David Armitage, *The Declaration of Independence: a global history*, Harvard University Press, Cambridge, 2007, p. 77.

12 The full letter can be read at www.stanford.edu/group/King/frequentdocs/birmingham.pdf

13 Edward Said, 'The Politics of Knowledge', in Paul Berman (ed.), *Debating PC: the controversy over political correctness on college campuses*, Dell Publishing, New York, 1992, p. 178.

14 In Edward Stourton, *It's a PC World: what it means to live in a land gone politically correct*, Hodder & Stoughton, London, 2008, p. 27.

15 Berman, op. cit., p. 22.

16 See for example Malcolm Bradbury's novel *The History Man* (1975).

17 For an elegant study of anti-harassment politics, and of one case in particular, see Helen Garner's *The First Stone: some questions about sex and power* (1995).

18 Daphne Patai, *Heterophobia: sexual harassment and the future of feminism*, Rowman & Littlefield, Lanham, 1998, p. 204.

   The Foundation for Individual Rights in Education, which campaigns for free speech in academia, suggests that anti-harassment policies now function as de facto speech codes. According to its President, Greg Lukianoff, a Stanford Law graduate (and consummate liberal), the US university is now a 'parallel dimension' in which the First Amendment doesn't appear to apply. His book, *Unlearning Liberty* (2012), is full of examples of proscribed behaviour, such as the case of a student at Indiana University who was disciplined for 'openly reading' a book on the history of the Ku Klux Klan. Of course, when universities start disciplining students for reading anything, you have to wonder what on earth is going on; but that this particular book was an analysis of the Klan's defeat (in 1924) in a fight with students from Notre Dame University adds more than a little piquancy to this tale.

19 Robert Hughes, *Culture of Complaint: the fraying of America*, Oxford University Press, New York, 1993, p. 24.

20 Catharine R. Stimpson, 'On Differences', in Berman, op. cit., p. 41.

21 ibid., p. 45.

22 The British novelist David Lodge is a fine *pasticheur* of critical trends.

In *Small World* (1984), he describes an MLA forum on 'The Function of Criticism' in which it falls to one Fulvia Morgana to articulate this approach to literature: '[She] said that the function of criticism was to wage undying war on the very concept of "literature" itself, which was nothing more than an instrument of bourgeois hegemony, a fetishistic reification of so-called aesthetic values erected and maintained through an elitist educational system in order to conceal the brutal facts of class oppression under industrial capitalism.'

23 Irving Howe, 'The Value of the Canon', in Berman, op. cit., p. 166.

24 In *Small World*, Lodge puts *this* approach to criticism into the (unstoppable) mouth of Siegfried von Tirpitz: '[He] said that, while he sympathized with the scientific spirit in which his French [structuralist] colleague approached the difficult question of defining the essential function of criticism in both its ontological and teleological aspects, he was obliged to point out that the attempt to derive such a definition from the formal properties of the literary art-object as such was doomed to failure, since such art-objects enjoyed only an as it were virtual existence until they were realized in the mind of a reader. (When he reached the word "reader" he thumped the table with his black-gloved fist.)'

25 Gavin Kitching, *The Trouble with Theory: the educational costs of postmodernism*, Allen & Unwin, Sydney, 2008, p. 37. Subsequent quotation, 'have been led down the path …', ibid.

26 Matt Cartmill, 'Oppressed by Evolution', *Discover Magazine*, March 1998.

27 The following passage will give the gist: 'Just as liberal feminists are frequently content with a minimal agenda of legal and social equality for women and "pro-choice", so liberal (and even some socialist) mathematicians are often content to work within the hegemonic Zermelo-Fraenkel framework (which, reflecting its nineteenth-century liberal origins, already incorporates the axioms of equality) supplemented only by the axiom of choice. But this framework is grossly insufficient for a liberatory mathematics.' See www.physics.nyu.edu/sokal/transgress_v2/transgress_v2_singlefile.html for the full article.

28 Jerry Holmes (ed.), *Thomas Jefferson: a chronology of his thoughts*, Rowman & Littlefield, Lanham, 2002, p. 242.

29 Margaret MacMillan, *The Uses and Abuses of History*, Profile Books, London, 2009, p. 120.

30 Stourton, op. cit., p. 218.

31 Hughes, op. cit., pp. 130–131.

32 Diane Ravitch, 'Multiculturalism: E Pluribus Plures', in Berman, op. cit, p. 287.

33 ibid.

34 Arthur M. Schlesinger Jr, *The Disuniting of America: reflections on a multicultural society*, W. W. Norton, New York, 1998, p. 93.

35 Diane Ravitch, *The Language Police: how pressure groups restrict what students learn*, Knopf, New York, 2007, op. cit, p. 3.

36 ibid., p. 13.

37 Hughes, op. cit., p. 134.

38 Ravitch, op. cit., p. 147.

39 Macmillan, op. cit., p. 116.

40 Quoted in Walter Blair, *Mark Twain and Huck Finn*, University of California Press, Berkeley, 1962, p. 143.

41 A question, intended only half facetiously: would an edition of Jane Austen's *Pride and Prejudice* that referred to Miss Bennet as Ms Bennet advance either the cause of women's rights or of literary criticism?

42 That the politically correct approach to language is predicated on an overestimation of its power becomes obvious when we consider the 'euphemism treadmill': the process by which offensive words are replaced with less offensive ones, which in time become offensive themselves and have to be replaced. Thus 'Negro' becomes 'coloured' becomes 'black' becomes 'Afro-American' becomes 'African American'. This lesson is obvious: prejudice has a life of its own; it cannot be defeated by language.

43 Tony Judt and Kristina Bozic, 'The Way Things Are and How They Might Be', *London Review of Books*, 25 March 2010.

44 Hughes, op. cit., p. 18.

Chapter Three: Fighting Ire with Ire

1 In James Curran et al., *Culture Wars: the media and the British left*, Edinburgh University Press, Edinburgh, 2005, p. 97.

2 ibid., p. 97–8.

3 ibid., p. 100.

4 ibid., p. 105.

5 ibid., p. 99.

6 ibid., p. 101.

7 ibid., p. 104.

8 Peter Jenkins, *Mrs Thatcher's Revolution: the ending of the socialist era*, Harvard University Press, Cambridge, 1988, pp. 245–246.

9 Curran et al., op. cit., p. 106.

10 See 'Nursery Opts For "Rainbow" Sheep', *BBC News*, 7 March 2006. Neverthless, this explanation of events didn't stop David and Gavin Mortimer from calling their 2007 book on political correctness *Baa Baa Rainbow Sheep*.

11 See '"Racist" Baa Baa Black Sheep Put Out to Pasture', *The Sunday Mail*, 27 February 2011.

12 For a detailed assault on *Sesame Street* see Ben Shapiro's *Primetime Propaganda* (2011).

13 Ravitch, op. cit, p. 62ff.

14 See the documentary *The Secret Life of Brian*, Spun Gold TV, 2007.

15 Todd Gitlin, *The Twilight of Common Dreams: why America is wracked by culture wars*, Metropolitan Books, New York, 1995, p. 182.

16 Hughes, op. cit., p. 28.

17 Camille Paglia, 'Ask Camille', *Salon*, 1997, online at web.archive.org/web/20080411071450/salon.com/july97/columnists/paglia2970722.html

18 Allan Bloom, *The Closing of the American Mind: how higher education has failed democracy and impoverished the souls of today's students*, Simon & Schuster, New York, 1987, p. 38.

19 ibid., p. 78.

20 Saul Bellow's final novel, *Ravelstein*, is an undisguised portrait of Professor Bloom, with whom Bellow taught at the University of Chicago, and doesn't stint at describing his preferences.

21 Michael Berubé, 'Public Image Limited: political correctness and the media's big lie', in Berman, op. cit., p. 130.

22 A good example of this is D'Souza's 'analysis' of Stanford University's decision to replace its Western Culture module with a module entitled 'Culture, Ideas, Values' (or CIV). Singling out one particular text as supposedly typical of the general tendency — a book called *I, Rigoberta Menchú*, by a Guatemalan Indian woman who'd become something of a *cause célèbre* on the left — he dismisses the entire module as hopelessly politicised. What he neglects to mention is that this autobiography is just one of 40 books on the course, which is itself just one of eight possible courses within the CIV module. (Incidentally, other authors on the 'Menchú' course include Shakespeare, Aristotle, Homer, and that incorrigible lefty Virginia Woolf.)

23 Roger Kimball, *The Rape of the Masters: how political correctness sabotages art*, Encounter Books, Jackson, 2008, p. 9.

24 Ravitch, op. cit., p. 136.

25 W. E. H. Stanner, 'After the Dreaming', in *The Dreaming and Other Essays*, Black Inc., Melbourne, 2011, p. 189.

26 Geoffrey Blainey, Sir John Latham Memorial Lecture, 1993.

27 In Stuart MacIntyre and Anna Clark, *The History Wars*, Melbourne University Press, Melbourne, 2003, p. 137.

28 Lyndall Ryan, 'Who Is the Fabricator?', in Robert Manne (ed.),

Whitewash: on Keith Windschuttle's fabrication of Australian history, Black Inc., Melbourne, 2003, p. 233.

29 Keith Windschuttle, *The Fabrication of Aboriginal History Vol 1: Van Diemen's Land 1803–1847*, Macleay Press, Sydney, 2002, pp. 402.

30 Keith Windschuttle, 'Introduction', in *The Killing of History: how a discipline is being murdered by literary critics and social theorists*, Macleay, Paddington, 1994.

31 Keith Windschuttle, 'The Break-up of Australia', *Quadrant*, September 2000, online at www.sydneyline.com/Breakup%20of%20Australia.htm

32 Keith Windschuttle, *The Fabrication of Aboriginal History Vol 1*, op. cit., Macleay Press, Sydney, 2002, pp. 131–166.

33 ibid., p. 397.

34 Gerard Henderson, 'Campaigner Stumbles on Whitewash of a Racist Past', *The Sydney Morning Herald*, 7 December 2004.

35 Robert Manne, 'Introduction', in Manne (ed.), op. cit., p. 7.

36 In Windschuttle's essay, 'The Fabrication of the Aboriginal Death Toll', published in *Quadrant* in November 2000, he writes: 'There is one good, general reason why we should expect the eventual compilation of regional studies to produce a very much smaller tally of violent Aboriginal deaths than the twenty thousand now claimed. Ever since they were founded in 1788, the British colonies in Australia were civilised societies governed by both morality and laws that forbade the killing of the innocent. The notion that the frontier was a place where white men could kill blacks with impunity ignores the powerful cultural and legal prohibitions on such action. For a start, most colonists were Christians to whom such actions were abhorrent.' In *Fabrication*, he repeats this theory, and appends a grumble about the many critics — some of them conservatives — who described it as absurd. See Windschuttle, *Fabrication*, op. cit., p. 360.

37 Robert Manne in Manne (ed.), op. cit. 'Singing a song many people wanted to hear', p. 7; 'a scholarly masterpiece', quoted p. 9.

38 Alex Altman, 'A Brief History of the War on Christmas', *Time*, 24 December 2008. But help is at hand in the form of James Dobson's organisation Focus on the Family, which has sought to weed out those American businesses so in thrall to political correctness that they greet their customers with 'happy holidays' or neglect to put up traditional decorations. Dobson has published a list of retailers divided into three categories: Christmas-friendly, Christmas-negligent, and Christmas-offensive.

39 ibid.

40 ibid.

41 John Gibson, *The War on Christmas: how the liberal plot to ban the sacred Christian holiday is worse than you thought*, Sentinel, New York, 2005, p. xxvi.

42 In Arthur Goldwag, *The New Hate: a history of fear and loathing on the populist right*, Scribe Publications, Melbourne, 2012, p. 43.

43 Gibson, op. cit., p. xx.

44 ibid., p. xxii.

45 ibid., p. 160.

46 In Altman, op. cit.

47 Gitlin, op. cit, p. 199.

Chapter Four: Thou Shalt Not Judge

1 Quoted in Nat Hentoff, '"Speech Codes" on the Campus and Problems of Free Speech', in Berman (ed.), op. cit., p. 222.

2 John Donatich, 'Statement', *Yale Alumni Magazine*, November/December 2009. Read the full statement at yalepress.yale.edu/yupbooks/klausenstatement.asp

3 Henryk M. Broder, 'Threaten One, Intimidate a Million', *Der Spiegel*, 1 February 2006.

4 Kenan Malik, *From Fatwa to Jihad: the Rushdie affair and its legacy*, Atlantic, London, 2009, p. xi.

5 ibid., p. 27.

6 UN Commission on Human Rights, Report by the Special Rapporteur on Contemporary Forms of Racism, Racial Discrimination, Xenophobia and Related Intolerance on the Situation of Muslims and Arab Peoples in Various Parts of the World, 13 February 2006, online at www.refworld.org/docid/45377b040.html

7 ibid.

8 See Alan Travis, 'Whitehall Draws Up New Rules on Language of Terror', *The Guardian*, 4 February 2008.

9 In Paul Berman, 'The Thought Police', *New Republic*, 14 March 2012.

10 Stourton, op. cit., p. 119.

11 Frank Furedi, *On Tolerance: a defence of moral independence*, Continuum, London, 2011, p. 7.

12 Nick Cohen, *What's Left?: how the liberals lost their way*, Fourth Estate, London, 2007, p. 12. Cohen, incidentally, is one of the authors of the 2006 Euston Manifesto, the purpose of which is to reassert the case for a secular, internationalist left. On the question

of the left's apologetics for reactionary groups and governments the manifesto is refreshingly strident: 'We decline to make excuses for, to indulgently "understand", reactionary regimes and movements for which democracy is a hated enemy — regimes that oppress their own peoples and movements that aspire to do so. We draw a firm line between ourselves and those left-liberal voices today quick to offer an apologetic explanation for such political forces.'

13 Stefan Collini, *That's Offensive!: criticism, identity, respect*, Seagull Books, Kolkata, 2010.

14 Pascal Bruckner, *The Tyranny of Guilt: an essay on Western masochism*, Princeton University Press, Princeton, 2010, p. 16.

15 The comments regarding Hirsi Ali and *Nomad* appear in Hilary McPhee, 'Prejudice Confirmed', *The Sydney Morning Herald*, 17 July 2010; Nicholas Kristof, 'The Gadfly', *The New York Times*, 28 May 2010; and Timothy Garton Ash, *Facts Are Subversive: political writing from a deacde without a name*, Atlantic, London, 2009, p. 180.

16 Tariq Ramadan, *What I Believe*, Oxford University Press, New York, 2010, p. 38.

17 See Paul Berman, *The Flight of the Intellectuals*, Melville House, New York, 2010, p. 214.

18 Tariq Ramadan, op. cit., p. 3.

19 Barbara Ehrenreich, 'The Challenge for the Left', in Berman (ed.), *Debating PC*, op. cit., p. 337.

20 On the ABC's *Q&A*, 27 August 2012, footage at www.abc.net.au/tv/qanda/txt/s3570412.htm

21 Margaret Atwood, *The Handmaid's Tale*, Vintage, London, 1996, pp. 314–315.

22 Kenan Malik, 'Illusions of Identity', *Prospect Magazine*, 27 August 2006.

23 Amartya Sen, *Identity and Violence: the illusion of destiny*, Penguin Books, New Delhi, 2007, p. 157.

24 Collini, op. cit, p. 50.

25 Jasdev Singh Rai, 'Behind Behzti', *The Guardian*, 17 January 2005.

26 Morris' comments appeared in Emma Pinch, 'Rushdie Attacks Play Row Apathy', *The Birmingham Post*, 27 December 2004. Rushdie was one writer who despaired of the weak response. 'It has been horrifying to see,' he told *The Sunday Telegraph*. 'It is pretty terrible to hear government ministers expressing approval of the ban and failing to condemn the violence … It seems that the Blair government's ability to disappoint knows no bounds.'

27 'PEN is concerned about protests over the filming of Monica Ali's

Brick Lane', English PEN, 19 July 2006. Read the full statement at www.englishpen.org/pen-is-concerned-about-protests-over-the-filming-of-monica-alis-brick-lane

28 Germaine Greer, 'Reality Bites', *The Guardian*, 24 July 2006.

29 Salman Rushdie, letter to the editor, *The Guardian*, July 2006.

30 Collini, op. cit., p. 31.

31 Ravitch, op. cit., p. 35.

32 Jeff Sparrow, 'The Panic in Europe: Islamophobia and the right', in Elizabeth Humphrys et al. (eds), *On Utøya: Anders Breivik, right terror, racism and Europe*, Elguta Press, 2011, Kindle edition.

33 Christopher Hitchens, 'A Ridiculous Rapid Response', *Slate*, 24 July 2011.

34 Ehrenreich, op. cit., p. 337.

Chapter Five: Don't Tread on Me

1 See 'CNBC's Rick Santelli's Chicago Tea Party' at www.youtube.com/watch?v=zp-Jw-5Kx8k

2 Thomas Frank, *Pity the Billionaire: the hard-times swindle and the unlikely comeback of the right*, Harvill Secker, London, 2012, p. 3.

3 Dick Armey and Matt Kibbe, *Give Us Liberty: a Tea Party manifesto*, William Morrow, New York, 2010, p. 84.

4 ibid., p. 92.

5 David Limbaugh, *Crimes Against Liberty: an indictment of President Barack Obama*, Regnery, Washington, 2010.

6 I defer to Wikipedia: 'To tea bag is a slang term for the act of a man placing his scrotum in the mouth of a sexual partner or onto the face or head of another person. The practice resembles dipping a tea bag into a cup of tea when it is done in a repeated in-and-out motion. As a form of non-penetrative sex, it can be done for its own enjoyment or as foreplay.'

7 Armey and Kibbe, op. cit., p. 81.

8 Michael Graham, *That's No Angry Mob, That's My Mom: Team Obama's assault on Tea-Party, talk-radio Americans*, Regnery, Washington, 2010, p. 21.

9 Frank, op. cit, p. 123.

10 Graham, op. cit., p. 16.

11 See for example Limbaugh, op. cit., pp. 110–122.

12 Graham, op. cit., p. 47.

13 Matthew Continetti, *The Persecution of Sarah Palin: how the elite media tried to bring down a rising star*, Penguin Books, New York, 2009.

14 Frank, op. cit., p. 124.

15 Tom Wolfe, *The Bonfire of the Vanities*, Jonathan Cape, London, 1988, p. 724.

16 See Tom Wolfe, *Radical Chic & Mau-Mauing the Flak Catchers*, Picador, London, 2009.

17 In Alex Spillius, 'Jimmy Carter: attacks on Barack Obama fuelled by racism', *The Telegraph*, 16 September 2009.

18 In John M. O'Hara, *A New American Tea Party: the counterrevolution against bailouts, handouts, reckless spending, and more taxes*, John Wiley & Sons, 2010, p. 50.

19 Theda Skocpol and Vanessa Williamson, *The Tea Party and the Remaking of Republican Conservatism*, Oxford University Press, New York, 2012, p. 69.

20 For the full Restoring Honor rally, see www.youtube.com/watch?v=e TCAhmB_SY4&list=PL13F20D01FDE38357

21 See 'Glenn Beck: Obama is a racist', *CBS News*, 29 July 2009, www.cbsnews.com/stories/2009/07/29/politics/main5195604.shtml

22 Christopher Hitchens, 'White Fright', *Slate*, 30 August 2010.

23 In Goldwag, op. cit., p. 18.

24 ibid., p. 26.

25 See Peter Johnson, Jr, 'Obama's Sad, Surprising Words', *Fox News*, 27 October 2010, www.foxnews.com/opinion/2010/10/27/peter-johnson-jr-obama-bus-rosa-parks-republicans-car-ditch-slurpee. And here is Glenn Beck on his radio show: 'Well, but I mean, in the fifties people were still in the bus, they were just in the back of the bus. What is the difference? You can't sit in the front seat. Why can't I sit in the front seat? Why can't I sit in the front seat, Mr President? Why am I sitting in the back seat? Why are you saying you have to punish your enemies? Are we looking to settle old scores here? Is that what's happening, Mr President? Because I'm just wondering. It sounds like there is a time to settle old scores, which sounds to me like you're inciting people.' Quoted on the Glenn Beck website on 27 October 2010: www.glennbeck.com/content/articles/article/198/47184

26 In Goldwag, op. cit., p. 27.

27 AFP, '"Unacceptable": Robert De Niro in Hot Water over Race Joke', *The Sydney Morning Herald*, 21 March 2012.

28 Matt Latimer, 'Joe Biden's "Chains" Comment and the Racial Double Standard', *The Daily Beast*, 15 August 2012.

Chapter Six: I Feel, Therefore I Am

1 See the footage at 'War Hero Mocked by TV Show Hosts', YouTube, 28 February 2012, www.youtube.com/watch?v=A4S7LpiqMbA

2 Clive James, 'Postcard from Los Angeles: 2', 1979, online at www. clivejames.com/books/flying/la2

3 This 'dud root' comment was itself amplified by subsequent revelations in the press that Corporal Roberts-Smith and his wife had undergone IVF treatment. Needless to say, in the furore that followed, Negus' remark was often interpreted as a sly reference to this particular detail. Equally needless to say, it wasn't.

4 Jones was referring to Julia Gillard's decision to impose a carbon tax. In its 2010 election campaign, the Labor Party ruled out such a tax, but changed its policy in order to win the support of the Greens in the hung parliament.

5 See David Marr, *The Henson Case*, Text Publishing, Melbourne, 2008.

6 Carol Hanisch, 'The Personal is Political', 1969, online at www. carolhanisch.org/CHwritings/PIP.html

7 'Port Huron Statement of the Students for a Democratic Society', 1962, full text online at coursesa.matrix.msu.edu/~hst306/documents/huron.html

8 David Lodge, *Changing Places*, Penguin Books, London, 1978, pp. 192–193.

9 Christopher Lasch, *The Culture of Narcissism: American life in an age of diminishing expectations*, Norton, New York, 1979, 'a narcissistic preoccupation with the self', p. xv; subsequent quotation pp. 4–5.

10 Christopher Booker, *The Neophiliacs: a study of the revolution in English life in the fifties and sixties*, Collins Clear-Type Press, London, 1969.

11 Lasch, op. cit, p. 72.

12 Kahlil Gibran, *The Treasured Writings of Kahlil Gibran*, Open Road Media, 2011, Google Books.

13 Furedi, op. cit., p. 156.

14 Hughes, op. cit., p. 8.

15 See Robert Bly, *Iron John: a book about men*, Da Capo Press, Boston, 2004.

16 Andrew O'Hagan, 'Celebrity Memoirs', in *The Atlantic Ocean: essays on Britain and America*, Faber and Faber, London, p. 158.

17 Frank, op. cit., p. 66.

18 Lasch, op. cit., p. 13.

19 Ian McEwan, *Saturday*, Jonathan Cape, London, 2005, p. 72.

20 Sarah Moore, *Ribbon Culture: charity, compassion, and public awareness*, Palgrave Macmillan, London, 2008.

21 Goldwag, op. cit., p. 281.

22 Julian Sanchez, 'Epistemic Closure, Technology, and the End of Distance', *juliansanchez.com*, 7 April 2010.

23 Leon Festinger, *When Prophecy Fails*, Pinter & Martin, London, 2008.

24 Clive Hamilton, *Requiem for a Species: why we resist the truth about climate change*, Allen & Unwin, Sydney, 2010, pp. 96–97.

25 ibid., p. 97.

26 Vartan Gregorian, 'Individualism and Civility: 2012 observations on de Tocqueville's 1831 America', *The Globalist*, 27 May 2012.

27 Brendan O'Neill, 'Tweet Police: censorship of the Tweetmob's making', *The Drum*, 30 March 2012.

28 As Clay Shirky has noted in *Here Comes Everybody*, many online irritations revolve around a misunderstanding of the ways that the internet redefines the concepts of public and private utterance. A comment intended for a particular audience is available to everyone, with the result that people may take offence at it, either because they lack the intelligence to put it in its proper context or because it suits their purposes not to.

29 Wei_Dai, op. cit.

30 Godwin's Law states: 'As an online discussion grows longer, the probability of a comparison involving Nazis or Hitler approaches 1.'

31 Adams, op. cit.

32 ibid.

33 Saul Levmore and Martha C. Nussbaum, 'Introduction', in Levmore and Nussbaum (eds), *The Offensive Internet: on speech, privacy, and reputation*, Harvard University Press, Cambridge, 2010, p. 1.

Chapter Seven: The Freedom to Offend

1 James Spigelman, 'No Right Not to Be Offended', *The Drum*, 11 December 2012.

2 John Stuart Mill, *On Liberty*, J. W. Parker and Son, London, 1859, p. 33.

3 ibid.

4 Thomas Paine, *The Age of Reason*, Prometheus Books, New York, 1984, p. 6.

5 In Lucy Hodges, 'Richard Evans: the don who's making history', *The Independent*, 23 October 2008.

6 In Clare Murphy, 'Irving Tests Europe's Free Speech', *BBC News*, 20 February 2006.

7 See *Schenck v. United States*, online at caselaw.lp.findlaw.com/scripts/getcase.pl?court=US&vol=249&invol=47

8 Ronald Dworkin, 'Even Bigots and Holocaust Deniers Must Have Their Say', *The Guardian*, 14 February 2006.

9 Patai, op. cit., pp. 179–180.

10 Milton, op. cit., p. 118.

11 Stanley Fish, 'There's No Such Thing as Free Speech, and It's a Good Thing, Too', in Berman (ed.), *Debating PC*, op. cit., p. 232.

12 ibid., p. 233.
13 ibid., pp. 244–245.
14 ibid., p. 245.
15 Collini, op. cit., p. 11.
16 Jeremy Waldron, *The Harm in Hate Speech*, Harvard University Press, Cambridge, 2012, p. 120.
17 George Kateb, *Human Dignity*, Belknap Press, Cambridge, 2011, p. 11.
18 Collini, op. cit., p. 32.
19 William Hazlitt, 'Number 387', *Characteristics, in the manner of Rochefoucauld's* Maxims, 1823.
20 Furedi makes this point in *On Tolerance*, op. cit.

Epilogue: Is Nothing Sacred?

1 The paper had form. In 2011 it landed itself in trouble with a special number, 'Charia Hebdo', which cited Muhammad as its editor-in-chief and bore on its cover a caricature of the Prophet and the words '100 lashes if you don't die of laughter!' In November of that year its offices were firebombed in apparent retaliation for the issue.
2 Leading the UK pack, as usual, was *The Independent*'s Yasmin Alibhai-Brown, who flew into print with an article entitled, 'Where's the 'Freedom'' in the Freedom to Abuse'. It began, 'Freedom of expression in the West is hokum, I say. It's hypocrisy dressed up as high virtue. Worse still, it is now used as a missile aimed mainly at Muslims.'

Acknowledgements

All books are collaborations, and since my name appears a number of times, in biggish letters, on the front cover of this one, I'm especially cognisant of the debt I owe to those who have helped me to research and write it. In particular, I would like to thank John King, for his unfailing good sense and support and for keeping me abreast of events in the old country; Angus Fookes, for his thoughts on the cultural evolution of offence; Simon Sparks, for his insight into the politics of offence as they operate on US campuses; and Dylan Evans, for his recommendations and his willingness to share his own experiences. I'd also like to thank Gideon Haigh for agreeing to read the manuscript, and for his very generous remarks about it. (These are now filed under 'Praise from Caesar'.)

Melanie Ostell has been a great source of encouragement and advice over the last two years, and I thank her for her friendship and guidance. Thanks, too, are due to Sally Heath, publisher of *Meanjin*, who agreed to publish my essay 'Offence Goes Viral' — the bean from which this book grew up and the bait with which I landed the commission to write it — and to *The Australian*'s literary editor Stephen Romei, who not only sang that essay's praises in his newspaper column 'A Pair of Ragged Claws' but who also contrived to augment my research (and keep me in wine) with several commissions relevant to the topic assayed in these pages. I've always been lucky with my editors, but Stephen's support has been invaluable.

Finally, I want to thank Scribe Publications, in particular its founder, Henry Rosenbloom, for backing a horse untested over distance, and its non-fiction editor Julia Carlomagno, whose meticulous attention to tone and content has enhanced the text no end. Needless to say, any mistakes and infelicities that have survived the whirl of her blue pencil are my responsibility entirely.